HAUNTED
SOUTHERN
MARYLAND

HAUNTED SOUTHERN MARYLAND

DAVID W. THOMPSON

HAunted
America

Published by Haunted America
A division of The History Press
Charleston, SC
www.historypress.com

Copyright © 2019 by David W. Thompson
All rights reserved

Front cover: photo from author's collection.
Back cover: photo from author's collection; *inset*: photo courtesy of Greg Knott.

First published 2019

Manufactured in the United States

ISBN 9781467144490

Library of Congress Control Number: 2019943509

I dedicate this book to my wife, Terry, for her patience with my minimal interaction during this process and to many friends and family members who've incited my interest over the years. They've provided incentive always, some even after their demise.

CONTENTS

Contents

PREFACE

Southern Maryland is a land of cultural diversity. From the old-world charm and anachronisms of the Old Order Mennonite farms in Loveville to the futuristic United States Navy test programs scouring our skies, it's a community in transition. In the span of a few decades, the rural heritage of the area has been transformed. Many centuries-old family farms no longer feel the caress of the self-reliant farmer's plow as housing developments and strip malls spring up to accommodate the influx of people and technology. Hardworking, independent watermen become rarer and rarer as the shorelines become dotted with the mansions of the affluent newcomers.

Local family names, once known by all, were trusted or reviled based on their antecedents. Loyalties or feuds were solidified by centuries of shared association. This quantitative certainty gave way to new "devils or angels" unknown. The fresh wave of interlopers rocked the local inhabitants as surely as the European invasion did to the native population nearly four centuries ago.

I'm told it's the same everywhere, this melting pot of American culture. But few places have experienced such rapid societal change as evidenced here, nor the dramatic culture clash of dissimilar mores and backgrounds. We all cling to the familiar, the comforts of hearth and home—even as a way of life disappears. Can the current fascination with the macabre, spectral ancestors and spiritualism be our desperate attempt to reconnect with a dying way of life?

ACKNOWLEDGEMENTS

My thanks to the many visitors and proprietors of the sites listed herein. Their tales add to the flavor and texture of the historical record. Kellie S. Hinkle, chief of tourism, Department of Recreation, Parks & Tourism of Charles County, and Sharol Yeatman, the external relations manager at Historic St. Mary's City, were very helpful and responsive.

I appreciate the many shared personal experiences and legends from (in order of interview) park maintenance program supervisor Greg Knott, Terry Thompson, Debbie Ammonn, Penny Bailey, Travis Farrell, Angie Farr, Debbie Yowaiski Dietrich, Matt Reimers, Robin Yowaiski and Sidney Wood. Their shared stories were invaluable (and more than a bit scary). Their insights and family stories involved many of the included locales and personalities, and their honesty, generosity and trust are cherished. Many others have contributed their accounts but wanted to remain anonymous. I've respected their wishes, and their input is equally appreciated. Special thanks also to Jayne C. Walsh (of Saint Clement's Island and Piney Point Lighthouse Museums) for providing the impetus for this effort. I'd also like to note my appreciation to my editor, Rick Delaney, for his valuable insights and sharp eye. Last but not least, my gratitude to The History Press for these intriguing glimpses of history in an entertaining format. The "Haunted America" series literally brings the "past alive."

INTRODUCTION

Dubbed the "land of pleasant living" owing to its laid-back lifestyle, mild climate, rich fertile farmlands and bountiful rivers and bays, Southern Maryland also has its dark side. Less savory nicknames such as Maryland's "Barbary Coast" and "The Wild Bunch" give testimony to the lawless years. Its past and present include a long and robust history of ghosts, witches and…well, things that go bump in the night. The myths and legends of paranormal activity here eclipses that of the rest of the state and, for that matter, most of the country. It's easy to understand why this inequity of the dark and ethereal exists.

The area is the oldest European settlement in colonial Maryland, founded in 1634 following the royal charter from King Charles I to George Calvert in 1632. Cecil Calvert, Second Lord of Baltimore, followed up on his father's dream: to establish a colony founded on religious tolerance, where Catholics and Protestants could live in harmony.

The Maryland colony was kinder to the Native Americans than were its neighbors to the south in Virginia. The Conoy, Piscataway and other Algonquian-speaking tribes found a mutual interest with the colonists: protection from the aggressive Susquehannocks and Iroquois of the north. After the defeat of these warlike tribes, when the original occupants of the land became outnumbered, their new European neighbors were less hospitable. The natives soon abandoned their ancestral lands to the usurpers, but their impact echoes in the many place-names throughout the region, such as Potomac, Nanjemoy, Wicomico, Patuxent and Chaptico, to name but a few.

Over the centuries, mobs lynched the innocent; tortuous prison camps were born; wars of religious, economic and political origin bloodied our shores—all building on the cultural genocide of a twelve-thousand-year-old culture. These tragedies collided with the horrors and heartbreak of normal lives lived and left an indelible mark on the soul of the region. The land is a fertile breeding ground for myths and legends and for believers—the sowing of the shadowy things we're afraid to look at in the eye. But be brave....

The histories of the places mentioned herein are listed in chronological order—not necessarily of their origin, but of the likely time period of the event that inspired their initial "haunting." Only the most prominent and oft-repeated legends have found a home here. Most of these stories have been known to me since early childhood—many related beside a flickering campfire on a dark moonlit night as goosebumps rose on my skin. My research includes personal interviews and, wherever possible, visits to the actual sites to get a personal "feel" for the place.

I'll make no comment on the veracity of any of these tales, and I report the legends and mythology as they've been passed down through the years. For the more current experiences, I've relied heavily on eyewitness accounts. Whether you are a believer or not, this narrative will take you on a journey through the haunted halls of this historic region...and, if you tread lightly, deliver you safely home on the other side.

1

PRE-COLUMBIAN PERIOD

NATIVE MYTHOLOGY

Long before the tall ships ushered in a new age of European expansionism, a rich, thriving and diverse culture already called Southern Maryland home. The Conoy, Yaocomico, Chaptico, Patuxent and Piscataway were among the many Algonquian-speaking tribes living here. They cultivated the land, fished the waters and hunted the forests long before the *Ark* and the *Dove* made their historic landing at Saint Clement's Island, Maryland

Their religion was dualistic in nature, incorporating "good" and "evil" opposing beings. Ahone was the good god, always a benevolent steward of his people. Okeus was a trickster and a dark god requiring their homage to soothe his temper. It's said the natives found the English practice of praying to a "good God" very curious. For their part, Ahone received little attention, as he was always a good god and needed no persuasion to treat his people well.

It's worth noting that Jesuit missionaries used the God/Satan comparison to convert the natives to Christianity. It is also supposed that the male pronoun used to describe their gods was an English interpretation. Given the length of time Native Americans occupied the region, is it any wonder at the reported spiritual experiences associated with their culture? Can it be so hard to believe that a people who once thrived here, and for so many generations—stretching back further than their ancient oral traditions—should leave shadows of their past behind? Are the echoes of their lives imprinted on the fields, woods and rivers they once freely roamed, where they lived, loved and…died?

I've wandered the still woods and felt the reverberations of the ones who came before. On occasion, I've imagined I felt the touch of an unseen hand and the presence of another, and turned to see no one there. Voices have spoken that I assumed to be echoes in my head—in the same way a dream downloads what the conscious mind no longer needs. Twice when this occurred, I've looked down to discover a perfect arrowhead at my feet— reminders of our shared past and, I hope, a welcoming gift. But perhaps it is a mere coincidence? I prefer the thought that the enduring warriors of before are still with me on my sojourns into the land we have both loved and that they welcome my presence there.

Scholars estimate the Powhatan chiefdom as having a robust population of 12,000 in 1607. Its numbers dwindled to 1,000 by the year 1700! Likewise, the other primary group in our region, the Piscataway (Conoy) chiefdom, numbered approximately 8,500 when its shores were first trod by Europeans, but by the same year (1700), the tribe numbered fewer than 300!

We're well-schooled about how the new diseases brought in by the Europeans—cholera, smallpox and measles—decimated the local populations of a people with no inherited resistance. The viruses hadn't

Historic St. Mary's City. Representation of Yaocomaco witchotts at the Woodland Indian Hamlet. *Photo from author's collection.*

16

been seen on this continent before. But it wasn't only the exposure to the new colonists that transferred the sickness. Many were infected long before Europeans settled in their areas. Other Native Americans also carried it with them in their travels from village to village.

In 1608, Powhatan commented to John Smith: "You may understand that I, having seen the death of all my people thrice, and not anyone living of these three generations but myself." The horror of this disease-driven genocide is beyond comprehension.

The Native American tales are not dissimilar to those of other Stone and Copper Age cultures. Our similarities far outweigh the differences. It is not my intent to commit cultural appropriation by including these stories here, but a true narrative of our shared history, tradition and lore would be woefully incomplete without including the ones who came before us.

In truth, few Native tales of the region survived the European invasion, and every tribe had its own mythology, but some were more universally accepted than others. One such tale is that of the Wendigo. Likely originating among the tribes in the Great Lakes region, the Algonquian-speaking tribes along the Atlantic coast all had a version of this legend.

THE WENDIGO

The Wendigo is also known by many other names: Wee-Tee-Goah, Witigo and Witiko. Roughly translated, these names all mean the same thing—a "man-eating spirit." It is a semi-human creature with characteristics of a "possessed human" turned monstrous. Murder, insatiable gluttony and cannibalism are its calling cards.

Most accounts of the giant indicate that it can reach a height of fifteen feet. Its eyes glow yellow—even in the dimmest light—with a body covered in dark hair, except for the head, which resembles the skull and antlers of a deer. (In Native mythology, antlers or horns possess great power, especially if found on a creature that doesn't normally sport them.) Wendigo fur is thin and barely covers its skin. When attacking, its long red tongue slithers between curved vampiric fangs.

The Wendigo is said to be born when a human being resorts to cannibalism. Perhaps racked with guilt and shame, the person goes insane and is possessed by this evil spirit. Its skin turns a pallid gray in imitation of death (perhaps reflecting the death of the human soul it possesses).

Native pottery at the top with axes, a mortar and pestle, various points and a colonial-era clay pipe at the bottom. *Artifacts and picture from author's collection.*

Early colonists heard the natives' tales and accepted them at face value. They kept a watchful eye out in the deep dark woods of this new and frightening world. Anthropologists consider this a cautionary tale—begun as a warning to the native people of the dangers of gluttony and cannibalism. Cryptozoologists speculate that the Wendigo and Bigfoot are one and the same.

Whatever your belief, the Wendigo is known as the ultimate predator, its senses finely tuned to every nuance of its surroundings. Every rock, every tree speaks to this forest king. If a man enters its domain—especially an enemy of its tribe—it knows. Hiding is not an option. Although a lucky stab to the center of the chest with a sharpened oak stave might kill the creature, if a Wendigo adds you to its menu, you'd be well advised to ensure your affairs are in order.

THE LITTLE PEOPLE

Legends of a race of little people are prevalent in many, if not most, cultures, including Greece, Indonesia, the Philippines, the Hawaiian Islands, New Zealand and, of course, Ireland and its legends of fairies and leprechauns. We certainly cannot forget the images derived from *Gulliver's Travels* and the legend of Lilliput. These far-fetched and archaic fictional tales have been given a fresh look after recent archaeological finds. Burial sites found at Flores Island (on the eastern half of the Indonesian islands) housed small-statured adult humans. Initial speculation is that this new hominid species (three feet in height at adulthood) lived concurrently with *Homo sapiens*. In North America, there have been similar discoveries, including a graveyard unearthed long ago in Coshocton County, Ohio. And, naturally, there have been many legends.

The Native people spoke of a race of hairy "little people," often depicted with horns—perhaps as a nod to the commonly held belief that horns and antlers held mystical powers. These people were said to live in the woods near hillsides that they used to their advantage in spotting enemies of their kind from afar. Some bands dwelled among the rocks bordering large bodies of sheltered water, such as the conditions found around the Chesapeake Bay and Great Lakes regions. There they'd fish the bountiful waters, with as many as a half dozen fishermen in each of their small canoes.

In Delaware and Nanticoke folklore, these diminutive humanoid creatures were named Pukwudgie. J.K. Rowling, the British author, made mention of the Pukwudgie in her Harry Potter series. The name is also a descriptor. Henry Rowe Schoolcraft (March 28, 1793–December 10, 1864), the American geographer, geologist and ethnologist, translated this as "the little wild man of the woods that vanishes."

Indeed, legend has it that they can appear and disappear at will. Some Native lore claims they lure people to their deaths using magic or by shooting them with one of their tiny poisoned arrows. The Little People were friendly to humans, once upon a time, but some slight—real or imagined—turned them against us. After this, any interaction with the Little People was never favorable for humans.

Native legends speak of the pranks they play on people, such as singing and then hiding when an inquisitive person searches for the music's source. One of the commonly held beliefs is that the little people create mischievous distractions to thwart human efforts. If only their contact was limited to such shenanigans, but the trouble they brought to bear wasn't always the

Historic St. Mary's City. *Maryland Dove*, a recreation of a late-seventeenth-century vessel commemorating the *Dove* of 1634, which accompanied Lord Baltimore's original expedition to Maryland. *Author's collection.*

annoying tricks they were famous for. They've been blamed for kidnapping people, pushing them from heights and even attacking them with their short knives and spears.

The preceding legends are but two of the many that the Native Americans shared with the newly arrived Europeans. Their stories merit inclusion considering the long history of the people here. Scientists estimate that in the Chesapeake Bay area alone, there are at least 100,000 archaeological sites.

2

COLONIAL ERA

A CAULDRON OF WITCHES AND HAINTS

The witch hysteria was not exclusive to the 1692 trials in Salem, Massachusetts. Although not as extensive as the accusations to our north, Southern Maryland had its own version of this travesty. There were hangings—often at the hands of vigilantes—drownings and homes set ablaze. The names of accused witches Moll Dyer and Rebecca Fowler are still heard here, often in warning to children or repeated by the flickering flame of a campfire. What gave rise to a religious fervor that could lead to such injustices isn't certain, but the fact of its existence is undeniable.

The Maryland colony was founded on the principal of religious freedom, but in 1689, Maryland Puritans revolted against the government to protest Catholics being in positions of power. The Puritan army defeated the standing army and, savoring their victory, immediately outlawed Catholicism. It was another war fought over religious doctrine. The new government soon fell out of favor, and another governor was appointed by the crown in 1692. However, true religious freedom wasn't restored in Maryland until the American Revolution seasoned the nation with spilled blood.

From 1654 to 1712, twelve individuals were accused and tried for witchcraft in the Maryland colony. Of those twelve cases, the majority occurred in the southernmost counties. Other accused never received a trial and faced nonjudicial "justice."

As in other areas of the country, of those accused, 90 percent were female. John Cowman holds the dubious honor of being the only male tried here for witchcraft. Also, unlike most witchcraft cases in Maryland, he was convicted of sorcery against Elizabeth Goodale in St. Mary's County in 1674. He was led to the gallows, and the rope was tightened around his neck when a last-minute reprieve arrived from the Maryland General Assembly. In lieu of the death penalty, he was directed to "serve at such labours as directed by the governor."

The fear of witchcraft is well known in colonial Southern Maryland. Archaeologists have uncovered numerous "witch bottles" at the threshold of colonial homes. These bottles were filled with pins and other sharp objects and then were filled with urine. They were believed to keep a witch from entering the home.

It is curious that the witch trials here didn't (thankfully) reach the level of hysteria that they did in Salem. Some historians feel it's because Southern Maryland was a true frontier during this period and that its residents had no time for such shenanigans. They had crops to care for. They had families and livestock to protect from the encroachments of the wilderness. Were there idle hands in Salem, then? I'd think that the reaction throughout the colonies at the travesty of Salem Village also stayed those other colonies' hands in later years, resulting in fewer trials and punishments (those state sanctioned at least). Despite the tempering of fears, some infamous tales of Southern Maryland colonial witchery still persist.

MARY LEE

The British trading ship *Charity* left London in 1654 bound for St. Mary's City in the Maryland colony. Well into the journey, a terrible storm racked the ship. The timbers were beaten until weakened, and many leaks sprouted along its hull. The sailors felt the storm was stronger and lasted longer than any natural event should have. Surely it was witchcraft.

The diary of Jesuit priest Francis Fitzherbert states that an elderly woman named Mary Lee was the suspected villain. The sailors accused her of summoning the unnatural storm and petitioned the captain to bring her to trial.

As the storm raged on, the captain continued to deny their request for a sea trial, so two seamen decided enough was enough. They seized Mary Lee, stripped her and searched her nude body for "signs of witchery." They discovered a devil's mark—a protruding teat (likely a skin blemish) that the devil and his minions suckled from.

Cannon from the *Ark*, one of two ships bringing the first colonists to Maryland. It was later used to defend the settlement. This is on display at St. Mary's Courthouse. *Photo from author's collection.*

With no further ceremony, Mary Lee was hanged from the mast and tossed overboard with all of her possessions. The *Charity* docked safely shortly thereafter at St. Mary's City, Maryland

MOLL DYER

Perhaps no legend is as prevalent in Southern Maryland lore or more a part of our collective consciousness as the story of Moll Dyer, the accused witch. After three hundred years, Moll's name is still heard here, especially around campfires late at night or as a warning to misbehaving little people. A recent film is said to have been based on her life. If so, there were many inaccuracies, the least of which was planting her in the middle of Maryland's Alleghany Mountains in lieu of the true origin of her story—the tobacco fields of Southern Maryland. The Weather Channel aired a segment on

Moll Dyer's rock on display at Saint Mary's County Courthouse. *Photo from author's collection.*

her life, of course highlighting the impact of weather during colonial times. (Drought and extreme winter temperatures figure prominently in her story.)

The historical evidence of the life of the "Winter Witch" is mostly undocumented. Courthouse records from the late 1600s were destroyed in a fire. However, there's evidence of two Mary Dyers arriving in Maryland around this period (Moll being a common nickname for Mary at the time). A letter written by a colonist references "Moll Dyer having a countenance so ugly it hurts to behold her." Further circumstantial evidence includes a road named after her and, likewise, a small run that traverses what is said to be the original Dyer homestead near Leonardtown, Maryland.

Most stories associated with Moll state that she came alone to the colony from Ireland via England, but some oral traditions hold that she was accompanied by an absentee uncle or older male family member. Many reports describe her clothing as old and threadbare but originally made of high-quality materials, such as the nobility of the era might have worn. This seeming contradiction raises many questions about her ancestry and adds to her mystery.

The legend of Moll Dyer is considerable. She was renowned for her curative prowess and hated for her lack of social graces. A virtual hermit, she traded herbal remedies with local Native Americans, and it's said she enjoyed their companionship over that of her own people. These traits alone made the unattractive old woman suspect to the very superstitious citizenry. A two-year drought began in the late spring of 1695 and caused demoralizing crop loss. On the heels of this devastation, an outbreak of disease occurred in the colony. Already a social pariah, the blame fell on Moll Dyer. Surely, she was a witch! And what's to be done with a witch?

The colonial governor arrived at a local gathering in the village of Newtowne (now Leonardtown, Maryland). Intending to celebrate with the locals, shake hands and kiss some babies, his path crossed Moll Dyer's. Exactly what transpired between them is unknown, but shortly thereafter, the governor's children became deathly ill. Searching for a cause, the citizens of Newtowne pointed their collective fingers at Moll Dyer. Proclaiming her a witch, they demanded the governor's intercession. Aware of the ignominy of Salem from only four years prior, the official stated that there would be no official sanction against her, but he'd not stand in the way of their "due justice."

In the dark of the coldest winter night of 1697, a frenzied mob of colonists rose up against her, determined to see righteousness restored to the colony. Armed with flintlock rifles, pitchforks and axes, they set out for Moll's cabin, their way lit by many blazing pine knots. It's not known who threw the first torch, but in mere moments fire devoured the dry wooden structure. Somehow, Moll escaped her intended funeral pyre and fled blindly through the woods.

Several days later, a young lad was searching for his missing cow. He stumbled upon Moll's lifeless body bent over a large rock at the river's edge, frozen solid. When Moll was wrenched away, the rock bore indentations where one palm had rested and her knees touched. One arm was frozen in an upright position, some say in entreaty to a higher power, some say to complete the curse on her tormentors. The latter reasoning held sway on the populace. They said the power of her witchcraft engraved the marks.

The eight-hundred-pound rock now sits in the courtyard of the St. Mary's County courthouse with a simple plaque proclaiming it "Moll Dyer's Rock." Curious visitors to Southern Maryland report both curses and cures after touching the infamous rock. Perhaps it depends on how the individual interprets Moll's story, or perhaps she knows whether their ancestor was among those wielding a flaming torch on that fateful night.

Moll Dyer Road sign. *Photo from author's collection.*

Over the years, many reputable eyewitnesses have reported seeing the ghostly white figures of a woman and her wolfish dog spiriting through the mists along the small creek that bears Moll's name. Many photography buffs have snapped pictures of the apparitions and of the small stream, only to later discover that no image was preserved. Hikers, hunters and other strong-willed rational people have scurried away from these sightings, unashamed of their fear but reticent to share their encounters. Some of the residents of the area near Moll's old homestead have reported engines shutting down or the electricity on their ATVs going crazy. One prior resident stated that he's been awakened at night by the sounds of a mob and baying hounds—but when investigated, no one was to be seen. Wide-eyed drivers in numerous automobile accidents bear witness to the bizarre sights they claim distracted them. It is interesting to read those police reports.

If you find yourself in the most haunted county in Maryland, take a drive by Moll Dyer Road and take a glance at Moll Dyer's Run on your way to the old courthouse in Leonardtown. Once there, if you're the daring sort, check out Moll's rock. Does it initiate curses or cures? Could it depend on the mood of her spirit? Or is it the content of the visitor's heart? Give Moll's rock a rub to find out for yourself.

REBECCA FOWLER

According to the Maryland archives, on or about "August 31st, in the year of our Lord 1685, Rebecca Fowler, having not the feare of God before her eyes, but being led by the instigation of the Divell certain evill & dyabolicall Artes called witchcrafts, inchantments, charmes, & sorceryes wickedly, divelishly and feloniously at Mount Calvert…& several other places…did use, practice & exercise in upon & against one Francis Sandsbury & Several others…and their bodyes were very much the worse, consumed, pined & lamed."

Rebecca Fowler was, in all probability, the same Rebecca Logan who was transported from England to the colony in 1656 as an indentured servant. When her indenture to George Collins, a shoemaker and tobacco farmer, was finished, she was free to marry her love, John Fowler, another past servant from the Collins plantation.

The two newlyweds were frugal with their meager earnings and, in 1683, purchased a parcel of land they dubbed "Fowler's Delight." They did well with their new venture and even procured indentured servants of their own, one being the aforementioned Francis Sandsbury.

The origin and extent of the evidence against Rebecca wasn't disclosed in the public record. Did an argument between the two incite revenge? Or did an accident befall Sandsbury that he attributed to Rebecca? Despite the "Several others" named in the charges leveled against Rebecca, no others came forward to accuse her at trial.

Rebecca was a landowner, and Sandsbury was a mere indentured servant, yet the jurors believed his account. Society's (and the justice system's) distinction between the economic classes was pronounced, suggesting a preponderance of evidence against her. The jury stated its view but left the matter to the judge to decide, unsure whether the evidence presented was actual proof of witchcraft.

The order was given that Rebecca Fowler be "hanged by the neck until dead." On October 9, 1685, she became the first "witch" killed by authorities in Maryland.

The notable witchcraft "incidents" and charges in Southern Maryland were as follows:

1654   *Mary Lee, victim of mob rule murder en route from England (in narrative above)*

1658   *Elizabeth Richardson, hanged at sea by sailors on the* Sarah Artch

1665   *Elizabeth Bennet of St. Mary's, acquitted of witchcraft*

1674   *John Cowman of St. Mary's (in this section's introduction)*

1685   *Rebecca Fowler of Calvert County (in earlier narrative)*

1686   *Hannah Richards of Calvert County, found innocent.*

1697   *Moll Dyer of St. Mary's, victim of vigilantes (in earlier narrative)*

St. Mary's City

St. Mary's City is the site of the first European settlement in the new Maryland colony in 1634. It remained the capital of Maryland until displaced by Annapolis in 1783 (then called Anne Arundel Town). St. Mary's City was declared a National Historic Landmark in 1969 and is a well-known archaeological site. Along with a multitude of colonial artifacts are many from the Woodland Indian period and earlier. Recently, three lead coffins were unearthed here, thought to belong to members of the Calvert family. One is considered to be that of Philip Calvert, a colonial chancellor and judge. Lead coffins are a rare find for the period and speak to considerable wealth.

Both the re-created historic site as well as the adjacent St. Mary's College are prime paranormal spots. Included in the reconstruction efforts is a native village built to reflect the technology of the period. There's a Yaocomico (member tribe of the Piscataway) brave who's been seen on several occasions

Evidence suggests that lead coffins discovered under the foundation of the original Brick Chapel of 1667 (at Historic St. Mary's City) belonged to Philip Calvert, his wife, Anne, and Philip's six-month-old male baby (from his second marriage). *From author's collection.*

roaming nearby trails. Observers have followed him, thinking him to be one of the reenactors who work there, only to have the young brave disappear on the trail in front of them. I guess he feels at home in the shadow of the longhouse resembling that of his people from centuries past.

Spirits attired in seventeenth-century garb make frequent appearances. Like the Yaocomico brave, they're spotted along the deserted trails moving to and from the different sections of "their" town.

If you decide to explore the grounds (and you should), enjoy the living history reenactments, the accurate reproduction of the *Dove* (the ship that first brought colonists to these shores) and a museum full of wonderful historical displays. A side trip to the Inn at Brome Howard (a renovated 1840s inn) might be in order. It's listed as a National Historic Landmark. As such, its history is long and complex. Perhaps a spirit or two resides there as well?

ROOKE'S LODGE

With the following, I've made an exception to placing incidents in an appropriate era, because the timeline of possible haunts stretches over a few centuries. I anticipate that its placement here will represent the earliest ones.

Rooke's Lodge is a private home located in St. Inigoes, Maryland, and has a very long history. Maybe long enough that generations of residents were unwilling to depart here—perhaps for love of home, family or both? As the property has been in one family's hands for generations, the ethereal happenings elicit intrigue rather than fear among the current earthbound residents.

The land that Rooke's Lodge sits on was originally part of Cross Manor, patented to Thomas Cornwallis in 1633. Cornwallis was very active and influential in Southern Maryland and served as one of the first commissioners in the Maryland colony. He held a captain's rank in the military in the early years of the colony's settlement. In 1635, Cornwallis fought the Virginian colonist William Claiborne over the jurisdiction of Kent Island and captured it in 1638. Five years later, in 1643, he successfully defended the colony against a Native American attack.

One would think that a man with so much vested in the colony would remain there, but fate conspired against Cornwallis. In 1644, Richard Ingle sailed the ship *Reformation* into the Chesapeake Bay and fired on St. Mary's

Reconstructed State House of 1676 at Historic St. Mary's City. *Photo from author's collection.*

City. (Ingle, a privateer, pirate and Protestant rebel from Maryland, joined forces with Captain William Claiborne to seize the colony from the Catholic governor, Lord Baltimore, in 1645.) Much of Cornwallis's land was occupied by the aggressors, and many of his buildings were destroyed. As a result of these losses of capital and colonial influence during the "Plundering Time," Cornwallis returned to England and died there in 1675.

The farm at Rooke's Lodge was sold to William Rooke in 1775 (it was larger at that time). That deed lists the prior names of the property as "Thompson's Purchase" and "Mary Taylor's Plantation." At that time, the house had four chimneys, two on each end. In the mid-1800s, the original house burned and only half of it was rebuilt; it still stands today. Currently, there is a chimney on each end (dating back to at least 1775). The middle section of the brick home dates to the mid-1800s. In 1980, the house was fully renovated and two wings were added to each end, along with a den and a porch on the back.

The following stories were related to me by the current resident of the home. I found her to be forthright and sincere, the progeny of an old Southern Maryland family line and understandably proud of her antecedents. She indicated that the earliest recollection she had of anything "peculiar" was when she was only nine years old. Her eleven-year-old brother and her seven-year-old best friend were also in attendance to bear witness to the events that follow. Her grandmother was babysitting that day, and the three children were settling in to sleep in the "blue room" (said to be the most haunted part of the home). She and her friend were in bed, and the brother made do with a sleeping bag on the floor. A whistling sound was heard that disturbed their slumbers. They ignored it at first, but the whistling increased in volume and tempo until childhood fear overrode any sense of youthful independence. They rushed to wake the grandmother. Instantly attentive, although I suspect still groggy from sleep, the grandmother hurried to their aid to discover the window cracked open a sliver, allowing the shrieking wind to creep through. She shut the window and went back to bed, assuring the youngsters that all was well. A few hours later, the three children woke again to the whistling sound, even louder this time, and again dashed off to wake the grandmother. She came in to find the window cracked open a second time! No stranger to the odd occurrences in the home, but no doubt cautious with her young charges there, she called her sister's husband to come spend the rest of the night for moral support.

It was shortly after her grandmother passed that the current resident moved into the family home with her fiancé. Now, the fiancé is a skeptic by nature, but that said, they both seriously considered leaving on one particular night. She was in the blue room putting clothes away, and as she passed by her grandmother's old room, she noticed the Bible that the matriarch always kept by her bed was disturbed. The Bible had been left as it was since the time of her grandmother's death, and it held serious sentimental value, so to find it left open was disconcerting. The fiancé was in the bathroom at the time, and as she noticed the open Bible, she yelled down the hall.

"Hey, did you open my grandmother's Bible?"

"No," he replied. "Why would I do that?" At the moment of his response, the lights died in her grandmother's room. She rushed toward the bathroom where her significant other was—just as the lights died in the bathroom… and in the hallway as well. I'd bet nobody has ever "dethroned the throne" as quickly as he did that night, literally jumping off the toilet, and they both dashed outside. While they stood staring at the house, the lights flicked back on. She felt confident that her grandmother was perturbed by their cohabitation prior to their nuptials.

About a year ago, and now sleeping in the grandmother's room, they were falling asleep and heard a loud bang in the wall behind their headboard (the wall separating them from the blue room). This was followed by the sound of something heavy being dragged down the hallway. Needless to say, it scared her enough that she instinctively drew the covers over her head.

"What was that?" her fiancé asked.

They crawled out of bed and spent the night downstairs. (She didn't say, but I'd imagine they got little sleep and kept their ears wide open!)

Her father had often stayed at the house with her grandmother at night. He'd reported hearing footsteps during the night on one of the staircases, and recently she had a similar experience. On a different staircase, again through the wall behind their headboard, she also heard footsteps. Her initial reaction was that it was her heavy-footed fiancé up to use the bathroom. It was about 2:00 a.m., and she reached over to find him in bed beside her. Checking further, she determined that both of the dogs and cat were present as well. She didn't sleep the rest of the night, but in an effort to do so, she persuaded her fiancé to swap sides on the bed. There were no additional disturbances that night.

When her grandmother lived by herself, which she did for years, she got locked into the bathroom (from the outside). She was forced to spend the night in the shower. When she didn't make it to her scheduled hair appointment, they came and found her. The doorknob had to be removed to free her from her overnight prison.

A few months back, our resolute resident went to check on her young daughter before retiring…but was unable to—she was locked out! The nursery room is adjacent to the bathroom where her grandmother experienced being locked in. Assistance was rendered by a coworker at 2:00 a.m. to remove the doorknob and lock. Far from an isolated incident, some of her friends have also found themselves locked in various rooms in the house.

Her father recently brought a stain to her attention. It was a bloodstain under the carpet, upstairs, that supposedly came from a sheep being slaughtered there. One must ask why a sheep was dragged upstairs to perform the deed in the first place, but she sincerely hopes it was indeed a sheep, and she intends to investigate further.

Many have borne witness to doors slamming for no apparent reason (and there are a lot of doors). She assures me she didn't say "slam" for effect, but in fact the doors bang shut violently, even on calm days devoid of breezes or drafts. She has friends who refuse to sleep in the blue room, and some have left in the middle of the night while staying there. Her brother won't stay at all. Perhaps the family cemetery in the backyard is only a part-time resting place for past residents' spirits and their ancestral home draws them back to interact with the living?

The purveyor of these paranormal tales says they always search for rational explanations for these events, but sometimes…well, sometimes, it's as Sherlock Holmes said, "When you have eliminated the impossible, whatever remains, however improbable, must be the truth."

3

AMERICAN REVOLUTION

TYRANNY'S END

No major battles of the Revolution were fought on Southern Maryland soil, but the state's soldiers who fought for independence certainly distinguished themselves as among the premier regiments. General George Washington was extremely impressed with the Maryland regulars, nicknaming them the "Maryland Line" after their actions at the Battle of Long Island.

On August 27, 1776, in Brooklyn, New York, a small contingent of Maryland soldiers (the First Maryland Regiment) showed England (and the world) what determination and courage under fire meant. Realizing the American forces were flanked, they held their positions under heavy fire and moved forward to attack the British onslaught. The British forces led by Generals Charles Cornwallis and Henry Clinton intended to cut off the American retreat and overtake the main force beyond the front line at Brooklyn Heights.

In their first significant battle, as others fled, Marylanders charged. A regiment numbering only four hundred men assaulted an entire British division. Outnumbered five to one, they sent wave after wave against the superior British force. As they advanced, musket fire and artillery rained down on them, decimating their ranks. They fell back—only to regroup and come at the Brits again…and again. The British were stunned by the determination and grit of the small force nipping at their heels and causing such damage. The Brits redirected their efforts to thwart them, thus preventing their attack on the main American military force at Brooklyn

Heights. Six charges were led by American general Mordecai Gist before his command was effectively destroyed.

On a lookout post at the summit of a hill at Brooklyn Heights, Washington watched the action through his scope. He's quoted as saying: "Good God! What brave fellows I must this day lose!" Among the "Maryland 400" were volunteers from Southern Maryland. The Marylanders' supreme efforts allowed most of Washington's army to escape capture and death. General Gist made it back to the main army with a fraction of the soldiers he began the day with. On the battlefield behind them, 256 Marylanders lay dead or dying. Students of the Revolution concur that, without the sacrifice and determination of the Maryland regiment, the war effort would have been lost. Colonel William Smallwood of Charles County was among the survivors. He rose to the rank of general and later became the fourth governor of Maryland.

Maryland's soldiers clearly had strong motivation. The state's enlistment level was high, their determination in battle unparalleled and the reenlistment rates were extraordinary. Historians have determined that over 50 percent of the First Maryland Regiment's soldiers reenlisted at the end of 1776. Maryland fielded seven regiments and the First Company Maryland Rifles, the Second Independent Maryland Company, along with several miscellaneous militia units.

Maryland's contribution to the War of Independence wasn't just the blood spilled and lives forfeited by its sons. It wasn't just the widowed wives and fatherless children. When the French joined us in our struggle, its navy was tasked with patrolling Chesapeake Bay. A pilot and merchant from St. Mary's County, Anthony Smith, drew a map of the bay's inlets and rivers, complete with sailing directions as well as Gulf Stream guidelines. The French navy used a version of Smith's map during its assistance throughout the war.

The War of Independence served to overthrow the political elite, and a new political class rose. The nation was "ours," and eyes turned west to embrace it in its entirety. A few years after the war's end, a large group of Southern Maryland residents migrated to the frontier of Kentucky (in 1785) and were led by the St. Mary's County guide Basil Hayden. They carried with them many of the distinctive features of their old home, including a penchant for the card game "Pitch" (based on the English post-medieval variant "All Fours"). Recipes for stuffed ham inspired by the culinary thriftiness of slaves accompanied them, as did Basil Hayden's process for what would come to be called bourbon whiskey.

MAIDSTONE MANSION

Although the particulars about the Maidstone mansion aren't well documented, it's one of the oldest surviving homes in Maryland. Named after a town in Kent, England, it was built between 1683 and 1699 by Benjamin Chew, whose family remained in residence for over sixty years. It is of note that the home was used as a Quaker meetinghouse during this period. But outside of the historic interest and the intrinsic beauty of the place, it's a daughter of the Chew line who remains to attract and entertain unsuspecting visitors.

Although little is known of Ann Chew's life, or that of her newly minted husband, it's said that she met her death on her wedding day in 1724. History does not record the exact manner of her demise or whether the recently hitched couple was even able to consummate their vows before her untimely death. While that's as it should be, it is this mystery that's fanned the fascination with Ann Chew and Maidstone mansion for centuries.

A short story penned by one of the owners in the 1960s revealed the legend as it had been passed down through the years. Mister Earl Hicks's tale states that Ann's father threw a gigantic celebration in honor of his daughter's wedding. Friends and family gathered from near and far to participate in what was sure to be the social event of the season.

After the vows were spoken and the obligatory period of social interaction was completed by the young couple, our bride mounted her husband's horse and wrapped her arms around his waist to begin the journey to their new home. Ann was very demonstrative as they left, waving and blowing farewell kisses to their assembled guests. Her husband noticed how still she became as they left the gates of Maidstone estate behind, but he didn't interrupt what he assumed to be a touch of melancholy for having to leave her lifelong home.

Upon arrival at the entry to their new home, the groom asked his bride to dismount. Although her arms dropped from his sides, she made no move to comply. He twisted about in the saddle to check on her, and she fell limp in his arms—dead!

It was Mister Hicks's contention in his family's story that Maidstone manor loved its mistress as much as she loved the estate, and neither could stand the loss of the other. But was this the truth of the matter? Or was Ann a reluctant bride who regretted a hasty marriage only moments after the deed was done? Did her husband, in fact, pine for another and, so, hasten his widowhood? Or did some horrid tragedy rip apart the newly joined lovers about to embark on their life together? Surely the angst from any of these scenarios would make an indelible impression on the property.

Ann makes frequent appearances around the estate but is seldom seen within the confines of the home. Was she an undesirable daughter-in-law and shunned to the point of death? Or did she prefer the fragrance of the flower garden to the stale air of the indoors?

Ann has been nicknamed the "Gray Lady" for the long flowing dress she wears (her wedding dress?) and a veil that has turned gray with age over the centuries since her tragic death.

The mansion and grounds were added to the National Register of Historic Places in 1971. Maidstone is a private residence.

SOTTERLEY PLANTATION

Sotterley is one of the oldest plantations in Southern Maryland, with the original structure dating to 1703. The estate was initially owned by James Bowles; at his death, it was left to his widow, who married George Plater II in 1729.

Their heir was George Plater III, a famous Revolutionary War soldier who went on to pursue politics. He served in the Continental Congress and ended his political career (and life) as the sixth governor of Maryland. He served from 1791 until his death the following year. He still resides at Sotterley today, buried on the property, where he can enjoy a view of the Patuxent River and his beloved plantation.

It's George III who is most frequently mentioned in visitors' accounts of their ghostly encounters here. Some say he lived and loved for so long on his cherished plantation that he can't let it go. Nor can he tolerate noisy interruptions to his peaceful existence—especially in the upstairs quarters of the manor house. The second floor is known as George's haunting grounds. Unsuspecting visitors have received shoves from unseen hands there. George likes his privacy.

After George III's death, the property traded hands a few times in subsequent years. Colonel William Clarke Somerville purchased the house and grounds, then sold it in 1826. The Briscoe family took ownership and maintained it for nearly a century when the wharf at Sotterley served the area as a thriving steamboat import/export location.

Sotterley Plantation mansion. *Photo from author's collection.*

During the Civil War era, the Briscoes (like many families in Southern Maryland) were Confederate sympathizers. They sent three sons to support the Southern cause. The family continued to live on the property until it was sold in 1910.

Paranormal researchers and other sensitive visitors can attest that George III is far from the only spirit roaming the halls and gardens of Sotterley. Electronic voice phenomena recordings (EVP) have picked up voices around the slave quarters as well. Disembodied voices order intruders to "Get out!" There are also reports of the sound of beating drums. Scents of bacon frying and coffee brewing have assailed the nostrils of workers when the home is otherwise unoccupied. One worker reported hearing her name spoken on several occasions. Cold spots, electrical devices that cut on and off by themselves, spectral voices, crying sounds and shadowy figures....Sotterley is a virtual paranormal cornucopia.

The estate is now listed as a National Historic Landmark. The facilities are available to rent for events, and tours are available. A haunted tour is held every Halloween that's well worth the trip. Hope to see you there.

4

WAR OF 1812

BRITISH REVENGE, OR
THE REVOLUTION REVISITED

During the War of 1812, private homes and manors were used as target practice for British cannons. Many lives were lost on both sides of the dispute, including noncombatants content with their families in the false safety of their homes.

The obvious causes of the war were the multiple economic sanctions undertaken by the British to support their participation in the Napoleonic Wars. Americans were also aggrieved over the British practice of impressment, whereby Americans were captured and forced into Royal military service. This was brought to a head with the USS *Chesapeake* incident. In June 1807, the British ship HMS *Leopard* spotted the *Chesapeake* after it left its Norfolk port en route to the Mediterranean.

It was suspected that a deserter from the Royal Navy, Jenkin Ratford, was a crewman on the *Chesapeake*. The Brits wanted revenge against the upstart "colonials." The British commander demanded to be allowed to board the ship to conduct a search, but the American commodore refused to allow an inspection by an "alien" power. The *Leopard* responded with a barrage of cannon fire that killed three Americans and wounded eighteen more. The *Chesapeake* was then boarded, and a handful of "suspected" deserters were seized, Ratford among them. The humiliating attack on a U.S. ship in American waters infuriated the American public.

To address their grievances, the United States tried various retaliatory embargoes. These impediments hurt us more than Britain, angering American citizens and providing backing to congressmen like Henry Clay who already clamored for war. In 1812, Congress made it official and declared war.

In Southern Maryland, the British established a blockade of the Chesapeake Bay in early 1813. Private homes and residential areas were fired upon, and frequent incursions were made overland, with raids conducted throughout Southern Maryland.

In Chaptico, the British troops attacked private farms, burning fields, houses and tobacco barns. At Christ Episcopal, the British troops vandalized the church, dug up the graves in the churchyard and stabled their horses inside the church.

British troops landed at Benedict, Maryland, in 1814 and amassed for their overland march to Washington, D.C. The U.S. troops staged in Bladensburg were severely routed. The city of Washington was evacuated, and the British burned the Capitol and the White House.

They then marched on, with the intent of taking Baltimore. British forces bombarded Fort McHenry but were unsuccessful in taking the fort. Francis Scott Key, an American lawyer detained on one of the British ships, was inspired to write "The Star-Spangled Banner" as he observed the shelling.

By midyear of 1814, it was apparent the war was lasting longer and proving more costly than either side had anticipated. The Brits were stretched thin with the Napoleonic Wars. The Treaty of Ghent was signed on December 24, 1814, officially ending the war. A strong feeling of nationalism prevailed in the years after the War of 1812.

What follows are some of the paranormal events and locations associated with the era.

BLUE DOG HILL

The period of the initial paranormal activity or possession reported at this site is hard to nail down. Various retellings have called this the oldest ghost story in America, dating to 1700. Others place the date in the late 1700s to early 1800s. The first written account was in a Port Tobacco newspaper in the late 1800s. The reporter interviewed local resident Olivia Floyd. She provided the details of a tale she'd heard since childhood and stated that she'd personally witnessed a sighting of "Blue" in her younger years. Olivia and her brother were former agents (aka spies) for the Confederacy.

Rose Hill, site of Olivia Floyd's home. *Photo from author's collection.*

The "Blue Dog Hill" story (also known as Peddler's Rock) occurred on Rose Hill Road in the historic town of Port Tobacco, Maryland. It involves the love of a man and his dog. What could be less disturbing and more human than that, right?

The man was a soldier, freshly returned home after serving his country. Young and unmarried, the soldier was reunited with the dog he'd loved since childhood. (OK, let's stop here for a moment. The "man," the "soldier" and the "dog" are already too repetitious and vague, so henceforth we'll call the man Charles (a calming, reassuring name) and our devoted bluetick hound (better known than her master), appropriately enough, Blue.)

The reunion between man and dog went as such things often do: Blue barked violently at the apparent stranger as Charles walked up his friend's driveway. The friend was kind enough to care for Blue in Charles's absence, but now it seemed his best buddy had forgotten him. Charles's eyes misted over as Blue growled and circled him. She sniffed and stared as Charles held out his hand. When his scent touched her nose, she twirled, danced and jumped for joy...right into Charles's arms. He struggled to retain his balance under the weight of the large hound. After that, Blue wouldn't let Charles out of her sight.

Charles's friend ushered him inside, and he could tell all was not as it should be. The friend presented Charles with a small box.

"What's this?"

"It's from your uncle. He brought it over for you about a month before he passed away. Said there wasn't no sense in giving Uncle Sam a cut that he didn't earn, and you've done enough for this country."

Charles ripped off the tape and opened the box. Inside was a stack of $100 bills and legal documents. Charles got a little teary-eyed as he recalled the man who'd practically raised him and took him fishing and rabbit hunting since he was a little sprout.

"Can you get the old crew together? I'd like to meet up at the tavern tonight. They all knew him and I bet they all have stories. He touched a lot of lives, especially mine. I wish I could've gotten home when he passed. Tonight, we'll have our own wake in his honor."

ALCOHOL FLOWED, AND LIES were told out of respect for the man they all held in high regard. As the night transitioned to the wee hours of the morning, one by one, they bid Charles adieu and left for their homes. When the last of Charles's friends said his goodbyes and offered his final condolences, Charles guzzled the remnants of a warm beer and slid from the barstool.

"C'mon, Blue, time to go home," he bent down and scratched the sleeping dog between her ears. They walked the lonely dirt road toward home, Charles's military swagger now a stagger.

"Hey, stop right there!" The voice came out of the thick woods beside the trail.

"Who…?"

"Never mind who we are, just empty your pockets, soldier boy. We want to see that wad of hundreds you've been flashing around." Charles heard the click of a gun's hammer as two men materialized before him. Burlap bags with cutout eye holes covered their faces. Charles reached in his pocket and withdrew the cash.

When the taller man reached out to snatch the money, Charles grabbed at the barrel of the man's rifle, but his inebriated state threw off his balance. The thief retaliated by smashing his fist into Charles's face. The other man joined in the fun. Blue jumped into the fray, biting the aggressors several times. When Charles fell backward, his head landed on a rock, breaking his neck.

Blue renewed her attack, and the thieves turned their full attention to her. She fought bravely in defense of her friend and master, but she was no match for the concerted attack from two sides. The taller thief smashed the butt of his rifle across the center of her back. As she curled up at her master's feet, paralyzed and whining, the other man finished her off, smashing her head with a rock.

THE FOLLOWING EVENING, THE pair of rogues met at the familiar tavern. The small bar allowed eavesdropping among the patrons. The thieves listened in as two of Charles's friends discussed their concern for him.

"I'm sure Charles is fine. Probably still sleeping it off and that's why he didn't answer his door."

"Or maybe he ignored us because he wasn't up to another night of partying."

"Tell you what, we'll walk the wood's trail back to his house when we leave tonight, just to make sure."

The thieves exchanged glances when Charles's friends spoke of legal documents and a farm deed that Charles was rumored to carry—sewn into the lining of his coat. They drained the last of their beverages and stood as one, then hurried down the same path that Charles had followed the night before. They needed to hide the body—after they searched it. Untold riches might be hidden in the clothes of the dead man.

"Served him right anyway," the tall man said. "Him and his damn war about broke us. None of our wares are worth nothin' no more with no trade. Who's gonna buy 'em? The other broke folks around here?"

As they chatted away defending their actions, they turned the corner in the trail. There was a strange bluish glow where Charles had fallen. Thinking someone was there with a blue glass-domed lantern, they crept forward. But it was neither man nor lantern that confronted them.

Blue stood with her front paws on Charles's chest, growling defiantly, still protecting her friend, her alpha. Her blue-and-black-ticked coat emitted an eerie bluish radiance in the moonlight. Her eyes burned with a yellow light as she took a step toward them. The murderers took a slow step backward as both of their bladders voided. The standoff continued for several minutes… or so it seemed to the men. They took another step backward, then another, then…Blue charged, saliva dripping from her grotesquely elongated teeth.

A man smoking a pipe on his porch a mile away heard the echo of their screams, and it's said that, in the dark of a still night, they're still heard.

Although Charles and the two murderers were never seen again, unwary travelers have reported sighting a bluish spectral dog, still guarding her best friend's resting spot, most often on a night in February when the dire deed is said to have occurred.

During our recent visit, no spectral hounds were seen or heard. Most tales indicate the canine is active only on the anniversary of her master's death, and then only at night. Maybe next February? Care to take a walk to see for yourself? I'm sitting this one out.

RESURRECTION MANOR

"Kids will be kids" is a familiar refrain, and what transpired in Hollywood, Maryland, to three young siblings on three subsequent weekends illustrates well the price of ignoring (or trespassing upon) the dead.

In the 1970s, Resurrection Manor stood on a lonely stretch of land on Scotch Neck Road. Once a part of a huge tract of land granted by the Crown, the manor house stood testament to centuries of occupation. It was reputed to be the oldest structure in St. Mary's County and perhaps in the entire state. During a British shelling during the War of 1812, a cannonball blasted through one of its brick walls and rolled to a rest beside the fireplace. When the warship moved upriver, the residents slapped some mortar over the hole and went about their day.

No doubt many families who occupied the original manor could relate their own experiences with the paranormal, and there's plenty of local history that might support their statements. Despite the craftsmanship of the builders, time took its toll on Resurrection Manor, so that by the time of our intrepid teenagers' visit, it was already a hazard, despite being designated a National Historic Landmark. From the events they related, it's apparent the War of 1812 left its supernatural echoes on the land.

On that warm late spring day in the '70s, two sisters and a friend drove through the circle, bypassing the manor house, intending to spend the morning fishing from the point. The youngest sister (and the purveyor of this tale) suggested they investigate one of the abandoned houses on the property. Finding an unlocked window, they scooted inside to find a most unusual circumstance. The kitchen table was set with dust-covered plates, glasses and utensils. Coats, hats and jackets hung neatly from a coatrack by the door. Magazines were opened on a coffee table as if the readers had just stepped out of the room. The oldest sister spotted a pair of small hand-carved pigs and, knowing the place to be abandoned, slipped them into her pocket.

The pigs were installed in the center of the young lady's dresser at home. That evening, the sound of footsteps descending the stairs woke her. She sat up in bed, and the two little pigs fell from the dresser to the floor. Over the course of the week, this scene repeated itself several times, the footfalls on the steps not always accompanying the movement of the pigs. By the weekend, it was decided it might be best if the carvings were returned.

After their second visit, the siblings convinced themselves it was only peculiar coincidence, a trick of a settling house and a window draft, not at all a warning from the past. That evening, they met with friends and related their tale. With false bravado, a few cans of illicit beer and a few double-dog dares from their friends, they decided to investigate further—this time in the older house, Resurrection Manor itself.

When the teens descended on the old manor house, they didn't proceed very far, as they found the floorboards rotten and feared they wouldn't hold their weight. They needed little excuse to take their leave of the creepy old building in the dark of a moonless night. Their flesh crawled with goosebumps, and the hair stood up on the back of their necks—even before the spiderwebs brushed their faces. They hurried away with frequent glances over their shoulders.

The following weekend, the two sisters and their younger brother again drove to their fishing spot. As they passed Resurrection Manor, the lawn and field around it were filled with people. Black men toiled in the field, working around small tobacco plants with their hoes. Another man swung his axe, machine-like splitting wood. Women pulled weeds from a small flower patch and hung laundry on a clothesline the siblings didn't recall seeing before. Their children ran and played ball games in the yard. None of this might seem abnormal in itself, but the entire group of folks was dressed in period garb…turn-of-the-century attire (and it was a hot day).

The oldest sibling slowed the vehicle, and all three exchanged troubled glances at one other, but an explanation was soon reached. The county must be putting on a War of 1812 reenactment. A boom echoed across the low valley and confirmed their suspicions. It must be cannon fire from the river, just like during the war.

At the sound, they stopped the vehicle, and the actors also froze in place… and stared at them. The performers' eyes turned dark, and their brows furrowed. The teens felt threatened, and cold chills ran up their spines. The oldest sister bit her lower lip and told them not to worry, as "actor types" were known to be a little different, a bit odd.

Still, it was peculiar that the show wasn't advertised. Maybe this was a dress rehearsal and the actors didn't appreciate their intrusion.

The teen siblings enjoyed the rest of the early afternoon catching perch and skipping stones across the Patuxent River. When their bloodworms were depleted, having no other bait, they called it a day and returned to their parents' vehicle.

Driving slowly back toward Resurrection Manor, they hoped to catch a glimpse of the players engaged in their show, but wanted their vehicle to go unnoticed. Windows down, the car crept forward until edging past a clutch of cedar trees that blocked their view. The brakes were applied gently, but not quietly. A drawn-out, high-pitched squeal announced their presence, and the actors' heads jerked up from their work.

As if their play was choreographed, the reenactors rushed toward them as one. The woodcutter swung his axe back and forth in front of him as he cleared the small fence and drew closer. The young brother in the back seat screamed. "Faster," he pleaded. "They're catching up!"

A cloud of black smoke from the car's exhaust temporarily blocked their view, but as it cleared, the giant axe-wielding man was upon them.

"Go, go, go!" The axe swung in a vicious arc as the car tires threw gravel then caught traction. From the rear of the car there was a whooshing sound as the weapon descended.

The trip home was silent. Each of the siblings was lost in their own thoughts; each tried to apply some manner of logic to the experience; each questioned their own sanity—as they did for years after.

They rushed from the car when they reached their house. Their hands shook for hours, their heads pounded and the thought of food turned their stomachs. It was too much, it couldn't be real.…Yet all three swore it happened.

NEELD MANSION

Neeld Mansion is another historic property, located in Calvert County, Maryland, near Plum Point. It is considered one of the original manor houses in the county. It is also known as Leitchworth's Chance. The patent for the property was granted by Lord Baltimore to Thomas Leitchworth (also sometimes spelled Letchworth) on August 31, 1663. The patent included 1,100 acres, and the initial structure was built around 1790, with numerous additions made thereafter.

Thomas Leitchworth was an important man in the Calvert County community. A Puritan, he was a judge for the county and also served in the Lower House of the Assembly. Lord Baltimore's grant is said to have been a reward for transporting early settlers to the colony.

Historically, the estate could be placed earlier in these accounts, but the ghostly happenings reported here have their origins dating back to just before the Civil War. There are the sightings of a black dog with fiery eyes in the "Devil Steps" part of the property that have been passed down from slave accounts. The sounds of a spectral woodchopper have been heard late at night, and a ghost is said to whisper in the west parlor. Interesting accounts, to be sure, but the most famous haunting related to Neeld Mansion is the crying baby heard in the wee hours of the night.

The story goes that on one fateful night, the mistress of the house, a cantankerous soul at best, was wakened from her beauty sleep by a commotion created by one of the house slaves' toddlers. Many accounts describe what happened next. Some hold that a noisy argument disturbed her and that she ran out onto the third-floor hallway, accidently knocking into the child and sending him to his death. An uglier account says that in a fit of rage for her lost sleep, she tossed the child out into the hallway, where he fell through the stairway railing and plummeted three stories to the polished hardwood floor and his death.

A large portion of the estate dwindled over the years and with each resale. At one point, a good-sized piece was sold to Samuel Chew (member of the same family as Ann Chew in the section devoted to her story). By the time of the purchase by the Neeld family in 1895 (for $6,000), the lot's size had dropped to 263 acres.

Recent owners report no babies crying at midnight, and after the renovation of the manor in the middle of the twentieth century, the "wood choppers axe" has been stilled. Perhaps loose shingles or an errant shutter or two might explain this? The whispering ghost also remains silent since a chimney repair some years ago.

The Neeld estate was subdivided years ago, and many houses are built on the old plantation. Ghost hunting is a lot of fun, and hearing the old stories is intriguing. But even as you enjoy your pastime, please respect the privacy and rights of private property owners. Neeld Estates and Beach is privately owned by the Neeld family and can only be used by the residents and their guests. Anyone else is trespassing on private property.

5

CIVIL WAR ERA

BROTHER AGAINST BROTHER

The Civil War was truly brother against brother in Southern Maryland. Slavery on tobacco farms was less prominent than on the cotton plantations of the South but still intrinsic to the production of the so-called sot-weed. Maryland is known as the home state of many great black leaders, including Harriet Tubman, Benjamin Banneker and Frederick Douglass. I'd be remiss to exclude Mathias de Sousa, the first individual of African descent to settle in Maryland. He was in the group of 140 colonists who landed at Saint Clement's Island in 1634. Mathias was also the first person of color to serve in the colonial Maryland legislature (and, by extension, the first African American to sit in a legislative body in what became the United States).

The institution of slavery continued to fall out of favor here for moral and economic reasons. In 1780, an import tax of £500 was assessed for every slave brought into the state, in order to prohibit the trade. The feeling that slavery was wrong was also gaining ground here. Three years later, the importation of slaves was forbidden altogether in Maryland—almost twenty-five years before the United States Congress followed suit in 1807. (By the way, the term *followed suit* originated with card games like Southern Maryland's favorite, "Pitch.")

In 1861, just under 50 percent of Maryland's black population was free, representing over eighty-four thousand freemen (more than any other state), although none enjoyed the full range of civil liberties as did white citizens. But with strong cultural and economic ties to the South, there's little doubt the state—and especially the Southern Maryland area—would have seceded if Maryland wasn't immediately placed under military occupation.

President Abraham Lincoln's "divided house" was exemplified by the well-documented Shriver brothers of Carrol County, Maryland. Andrew was a slaveholder yet sided with the Union. His brother, William, didn't own slaves. He considered the practice to be morally reprehensible and convinced his mother to free her slaves as well. Oddly enough, four of William's sons joined the Confederacy. The political fervor of the war pitted brother against brother throughout the state.

In Maryland, political leaders were imprisoned without trials, printing presses were destroyed and Northern spies turned the land of pleasant living into a virtual prison. Lincoln's subjugation of Maryland defied the Constitution and presented onerous conditions to the entire state, and to Southern Marylanders especially. Martial law was imposed, and the right of habeas corpus was revoked. (I'm not a lawyer, but essentially this is the right of all citizens to report illegal detention when arrested and to be made aware of the reason for their incarceration). Southern sympathizers and government officials were summarily arrested.

In the November elections of 1861, Federal provost marshals "guarded" the Southern Maryland polls. Democrats and others known to be sympathetic to the Confederate cause were arrested. State judges, after the fact, directed the grand jury to investigate the allegations and were in turn arrested. These were the charges that Supreme Court chief justice Roger B. Taney took President Lincoln to task over in defense of his homeland. In response, the president issued orders for the chief justice's arrest.

In response to these transgressions, many locals crossed the Potomac to join with Virginia troops to escape the burdensome circumstances. To teach this border state a lesson, a POW camp for captured Confederate soldiers was created at the southernmost point of the tri-county area. The conditions at the Point Lookout camp were later decried as comparable to those faced at Andersonville, Georgia. Starvation diets of wormy meal, lice-filled beds in communal tents set on marshy ground and diseases from severe overcrowding (built to hold ten thousand prisoners, it bloated to twenty thousand by war's end) led to four thousand deaths, or an 8 percent mortality rate.

Postwar Marylanders (and Southern Marylanders especially) felt more isolated than they ever had before. The sentiment of the period was that Maryland was a people without a nation. It was a time when thoughts became nostalgic in nature, and it seems their ghost stories reflected that.

POINT LOOKOUT PRISON CAMP

From the lighthouse to the prison camp and everywhere in between, Point Lookout is the most haunted site in Maryland, if not the entire country, rivaling Gettysburg, Pennsylvania, for this dubious distinction. Its haunted history is even noted on state-sanctioned brochures and webpages, a rare nod to the paranormal by any governmental body.

Named during the War of 1812 for providing a watch post for British invaders, this narrow strip of land marks the southernmost point of the western shore of Maryland. It's formed by the confluence of the Potomac River with the Chesapeake Bay, giving it great value for fishermen, traders, vacationers—and, of course, warmongers. Indian massacres, lighthouse deaths, shipwrecks, multiple suicides and barbaric hospital and camp conditions during the Civil War period have amassed a large population of spectral residents. The POW camp provides the most fodder for the paranormal mill, and a large percentage of the hauntings date to this period.

In the course of the war, 52,264 Confederate soldiers were incarcerated at Fort Lincoln's Camp Hoffman. Many died of dysentery, typhoid fever, malaria, smallpox, starvation and murder. The exact number of deaths is impossible to pinpoint, as many prisoners were entombed in mass graves during periods of high mortality. One such period was May 1865 (three months after the war's end), when 324 men died in the thirty-one-day span.

Barracks were not provided for the inmates, only a sunken "tent city" nicknamed the "bullpen." Up to sixteen men were assigned to each fifteen-square-foot tent, with one blanket to share among every three men. Rations were starvation diets, and many inmates depended on rats for their source of protein.

Animosity was to be expected from wartime enemies, but Point Lookout was regarded as one of the cruelest camps. Included among the guards were United States Colored Troop (USCT) Regiments, but the brutality wasn't confined to the former slaves. In fact, many were stunned by the conditions their former masters were forced to endure. One former captive wrote that officers of the day often offered from ten to fifteen dollars to guards for each prisoner they shot in "the discharge of their duties" that day.

Park maintenance program supervisor Greg Knott has observed some of Point Lookout's secrets for himself. He tells of the maintenance building that was erected within the area of the prison pen. Late at night, footsteps can often be heard up and down the stairs. Doors slam when no other person is occupying the building.

Above: Camp Hoffman re-creation, Point Lookout State Park. *Photo from author's collection.*

Left: Point Lookout POW sign. *Photo from author's collection.*

Once, he spotted the mysterious Civil War–era "lady." Dressed in period clothing with a wide-brimmed hat, she walked across the road from the pen area toward the water. He'd seen no vehicle and wondered from where she might have originated. There's only one road in, and that comes to a dead-end circle at the point. He drove to the end and circled back to pass by where he'd first spotted her. He saw no one and no vehicle. Moving on, he met another park employee driving toward him. He stopped her and asked if she'd seen a vehicle—or the woman—but she stated that the entire park was empty and no vehicles had made their way past her.

The maintenance supervisor, his curiosity piqued, turned the vehicle around to retrace his route. Approaching the area, he spotted the woman silhouetted in the open area near the water. He turned his vehicle down one of the employee-only access roads that lead to the spot, the trees blocking his view of her for but a moment…and she was gone. Park rangers and longtime park visitors call the spectral lady Miss Courtney, someone who had lived at the point—likely before the war.

Many other ghosts are reported from this period. A one-armed Confederate soldier searches for his brother, while others hunt for their gravesites. One soldier is often seen crossing the road from the site of the smallpox quarantine unit. His homespun uniform is in tatters, and as he passes, the scents of gunpowder and mildew assail the nostrils of the living. This spirit does not speak and appears to be unaware of observers as he continues on his way toward the river and anticipated liberty. It's doubtful he made it to freedom during his lifetime. Towers with armed guards were strategically placed around the camp, and an iron-clad warship, the USS *Roanoke*, guarded against any escape via the water. Despite being surrounded by Confederate sympathizers, only fifty successful escapes were ever made from the camp.

Location of Civil War lady (Miss Courtney) sightings. *Photo courtesy of Greg Knott.*

Confederate memorial at Point Lookout. *Photo from author's collection.*

It was a common practice for nurses in the smallpox quarantine hospital to pinch patients' toes to determine if they were still living. Many overnight campers have been jerked awake in the middle of the night when their toes are pinched through their sleeping bags!

Along with the many sightings, electronic voice phenomena (EVP) have been recorded on the road leading from the river to the camp, voices saying, "He's in bad shape" and "Fire if they get too close to you." But most of the ethereal figures remain silent when encountering the living. Perhaps their anguish requires silent reflection, or maybe what they witnessed is beyond the scope of human exchange—whether dead or alive.

Point Lookout Lighthouse

In 1830, the Point Lookout Lighthouse was built in the aftermath of generations of shipwrecks. The energies of several Civil War soldiers, lighthouse keepers of old and sailors predating the North-South conflict frequent the building and surrounding area. With some regret, I found that the lighthouse is currently closed to the public while safety concerns are addressed and renovations made.

The site has been investigated by several paranormal television shows and, in 1980, by Dr. Han Holzer, a prominent paranormal researcher. Here the team found great success in recording EVP. Twenty-four separate vocalizations were picked up, including the following.

"This is my house," ascribed to Ann Davis, former lighthouse keeper and the first woman to receive an official keeper's appointment on the Chesapeake Bay. She was found dead in the lantern room after having completed her daily routine.

Other, less readily identifiable ghosts were recorded saying, "I was in the water." In another instance, a woman's voice suggested, "Let's take no objection to what they are doing." One voice pleaded, "Help us," and, later, a gruff older man's voice commanded, "Get off that pier." Sadly, a young child is heard to ask, "Can I play?" Several visitors to the lighthouse have reported the sound of pounding horse hooves approaching, but no spectral horses were seen by anyone I interviewed.

Visual phenomena are also well documented here. There's the man who stands silent on the lighthouse porch then walks into the wall and disappears when spoken to. A young lad, estimated to be about eight years old, has been

Point Lookout Lighthouse. *Photo from author's collection.*

seen. He's known to interact with visitors. Is it conceivable that he's the same boy who asks to play? On the beach fronting the lighthouse, multiple figures have been seen walking along the sand. They abruptly disappear when lights from vehicles or flashlights attempt to illuminate them.

Program supervisor Greg Knott shared some personal experiences he's had in and around the site. After Hurricane Irene raked the shores of the bay, the basement of the lighthouse flooded. As the water receded, he and another park employee entered the basement to evaluate the damage from its only access point, the interior steps. Although the water was gone, it left behind a fine, muddy silt covering the floor. Ten feet from the bottom step, they saw a series of disturbances in the mud and investigated. Footprints began—and, I reiterate, a full ten feet from the stairway. Such a jump would qualify for the Olympics, and the effort would have left sign of a slip at landing, but that wasn't the case. The footprints continued from there across the floor until the midpoint of the room, where they disappeared again, as if the walker levitated through the floor joists above.

One of the last residents in the lighthouse was Laura Berg in the 1970s. Accepting the presence of the spirits sharing her domicile, she felt no fear

58

and never considered that they meant her any harm. In fact, she suspected that the spirit of Ann Davis might have saved her life.

One night, as she slept peacefully, she woke to see lights dancing above her bed. She felt an abiding sense of dread and danger, followed by a strong smoke smell. She fled her bedchambers and descended to the lower level of the lighthouse, there to find a space heater engulfed in flames. Arriving before the flames spread, she smothered the fire in short order. Without the timely warning, however, she felt the outcome would've been devastating.

One notable apparition not falling within the Civil War timeframe is thought to be Joseph Heaney (Haney), the second mate of the cargo and passenger ship *Express* out of Baltimore. Unaware of the severe storm postings, the steamer ship met up with a coastal storm (named the "Gale of '78"). The severe winds ripped the deck off Heaney's ship, and waves ripped it to pieces off Point Lookout. Sixteen lives were lost, including Heaney's.

Local oral tradition holds that Heaney attempted to gain shore via rowboat for assistance from the lighthouse keeper, but because of the raging storm, he never made it to land. But that wasn't the last that was seen of him.

During severe storms, he's been heard knocking at the door of the lighthouse. On occasion, he's appeared on the beach in a sopping wet period uniform just before severe weather strikes, perhaps to warn unsuspecting sailors of the imminent storm.

On January 11, 1966, an era ended when the lighthouse light was extinguished for the last time. But it seems some have never left.

GREENWELL STATE PARK

Fishing, kayaking, crabbing, swimming, hiking, picnicking, hunting and even horseback riding are available here. What more could you ask of a state park? How about a chilling dose of the paranormal, because there's plenty of it here to go around!

Greenwell comprises approximately 600 acres and is located on the Patuxent River in Hollywood, Maryland. It was formed by combining a donated 166-acre farm (from John Greenwell and his sister Mary Greenwell) and the purchased Bond's farm of 430 acres soon after. The Greenwells' donation was earmarked for use as a public park. Both farms were once encompassed by the 4,000-acre grant to Captain Thomas Cornwaleys in 1650. This tract was originally known as Resurrection Manor (described in chapter 4). The park is jointly managed by the state and the Greenwell Foundation, a nonprofit organization devoted to accessible outdoor recreation.

Following the main entrance of the park, you can't miss Rosedale Manor, built around 1880. The mansion boasts a beautiful rose garden, and its location on the Patuxent River shoreline provides an amazing view.

The sightings of Civil War soldiers over the years—inside the private residences, in the woods surrounding the property, on the beaches and in the manor house—leave no doubt of the timeline of the major hauntings at this park. As attractive as this park is, it's not the magnificent flora and fauna that attracts students and fans of the supernatural. As Civil War centric as this park's history is, it's not a single disembodied spirit that frequents the homes and grounds, nor one timeline they represent. One particular phantom, however, is my personal favorite.

The stories that follow were related to me by two different people who lived in one of the private residences on the park. The first story was told by a teenage resident about one night he spent at the house in Greenwell shortly after moving there. The park offered plenty of opportunities for outdoor fun, as noted above, but it's when he turned in for the night that the real excitement began—at least for the young man.

He told me he woke from a sound slumber and felt a form of sleep paralysis. Now, science explains this phenomenon as being due to REM sleep being suddenly interrupted, and the young man stated that the dream (or, more appropriately, nightmare) was intense and involved children being attacked in the nursery room down the hall from him. That's when a figure swept into the room and he got a good look. Standing just feet away, staring at him, was a nun in the old habit style of dress. She leaned down and held her hands together in a gesture of prayer.

"Bless you," she said, and at her words, he could move again. She left as quickly as she'd arrived—perhaps to check on her other charges. He jumped from his bed and ran out into the hallway to find it empty.

The young man told me he'd seen the nun again outside by the horses, and once, while walking outside, he spotted her staring at him from inside the house!

Sometime later, another resident's brother and his girlfriend came down for a visit. They were relaxing on the pier and watching the approach of a storm across the river. Thinking they had plenty of time before the storm reached them, they leaned back and reclined on the weathered boards. As it turned out, they were too relaxed, as a high wave washed over them and

Greenwell State Park pier, Hollywood, Maryland. *Photo courtesy of Greg Knott.*

threw them into the river. The young woman was lucky enough to latch on to one of the pier's pylons. The brother wasn't as fortunate. Suddenly wakened, but a poor swimmer, he struggled against the pull of the water. Again, a wave struck that pushed him under, and he knew he was going to drown. As he fought the swirling sea in a last-ditch effort, he felt a hand on his arm pulling him up! As his head popped out of the water, he saw a nun wearing the old-time habit. She didn't speak as she dragged him to the shallows.

The brother coughed up the water from his lungs as his girlfriend pulled herself up on the pier. He heard the "thump-thump" of his brother's boots on the wooden deck of the pier. He lifted himself to his knees and searched the pier and shoreline for his savior.

"Where did she go?"

His brother shook his head. "Who?"

"The nun."

"Nobody here but the three of us. Are you OK? I thought you were a goner."

The nearly drowned brother and the teenager did not know of each other's experience. They'd not spoken about it, as they were hesitant to share their tales with anyone. So, when they went for a tour of the

This Greenwell descendant's portrait hangs in the manor house. Is it Sister Mary Estelle? *Photo courtesy of Greg Knott.*

manor house, they both received a shock as they admired the antique photos on the wall.

"That's her," the once waterlogged brother pointed at a displayed picture. "That's who I saw that night by the pier. She's the Sister who pulled me out of the water. She saved my life."

When the teenager beheld the photograph, his jaw dropped and his face flushed. "That's the one I saw, too! She's the one who was in my room!"

I'm sure science can explain this away—mass hypnosis, lack of oxygen in the case of the brother or sleep deprivation? I can't help but find it odd that two unrelated people (with no prior knowledge of the other's experience) would key in on the same old photograph, especially as one is (or was?) a nonbeliever about such things.

Luckily for the brother, one scion of the Greenwell family followed her heart and her calling to become a nun. Her good deeds apparently continue beyond our mortal plane. Her picture still hangs in the manor house at Greenwell. Although not identified, I believe her to be Mary Grace Greenwell, who became Sister Mary Estelle Greenwell. She was a nun in the Sisters of Charity of Nazareth order and was a sister to the donators of the manor home and farm. Mary Estelle lived from 1900 to 1991 and is buried in Jefferson County, Kentucky. It would seem her yearning for home never died.

DOCTOR MUDD'S HOUSE

Moving forward in time to the war's end and north on the compass, we find ourselves at the estate once known as Saint Catherine's, the home of Dr. Samuel Alexander Mudd—Civil War conspirator…or innocent pawn in a tragedy of historic proportions.

If Samuel had not honored his Hippocratic Oath on one fateful night, the good doctor's name would be lost to the obscurity of time. His reputation as a good and honorable man, a fine father and a faithful husband wouldn't ensure his name's immortality beyond the scope of a single generation or two, but his infamy would.

Samuel was born on December 20, 1833, in Charles County, Maryland, on his family's plantation (one that's remained in the family for over two centuries). He attended school at Saint John's College in Frederick, then Georgetown, and finally received his medical degree from Baltimore Medical College. Shortly thereafter, on Thanksgiving Day 1857, he married his childhood sweetheart, Sarah Francis Dyer. If Sarah was related to the ill-fated Moll Dyer mentioned earlier, their kinship is lost to time (and the destroyed records of a burned courthouse).

On the day that Dr. Mudd began his ascent to notoriety, he was thirty-one years old with four children. At 4:00 a.m. on April 14, 1865, actor John Wilkes Booth arrived with his traveling companion, David Herold. Booth's leg was broken in a fall and had swollen to the point that his boot had to be cut off. Samuel set the leg and splinted it and allowed the men to remain in an upstairs bedroom to rest.

Booth's next stop in his escape route was to the home of Samuel Cox in Bel Alton, Maryland, leaving there on April 21 and crossing the Potomac River into Virginia. Two weeks after Lincoln's assassination, on Garrett's

Dr. Samuel Mudd's house. *Photo from author's collection.*

farm, the Union cavalry surrounded the shed that Booth occupied and set it ablaze. He was shot in the neck and paralyzed as he tried to escape the inferno. He was dragged to the Garretts' front porch and died.

What additional role did Dr. Mudd play in the conspiracy, if any? We know that Booth's leg was broken as he jumped from the balcony at Ford's Theatre—after he'd assassinated our sixteenth president, Abraham Lincoln. Dr. Mudd stated that he was unaware of Booth's deed, yet he didn't report Booth's visit for twenty-four hours after he'd left the plantation. The doctor's story varied on a few components, most notably his relationship with Booth. The doctor maintained he didn't know the man, but testimony during the trial proved they'd met on several occasions and that Booth had even stayed at Mudd's house.

Was Mudd an innocent victim of the times and of his professional duty? He was a known Southern sympathizer, owned slaves and fell on hard times financially during the war. He'd met with Booth on occasion and set the man's leg. He'd even enlisted the help of a local carpenter to build Booth a pair of crutches. Only the doctor, his wife and the dead Booth knew the entire story. The former two pled his innocence until their deaths.

The courts, however, found Dr. Mudd guilty of aiding and conspiring in a murder. He was sentenced to life imprisonment in a federal prison—Fort Jefferson on Dry Tortugas, seventy miles west of the Florida Keys.

Mudd's imprisonment was uneventful for the most part. Rations of stale bread and rotted meat weren't unusual for political prisoners and murderers. He did make one unsuccessful escape attempt in September 1865. However, a yellow fever epidemic broke out in the camp, and the doctor's services were required. Mudd worked tirelessly by all accounts, as 270 people contracted the dreaded disease. His expertise saved many lives, and the epidemic proved fatal for only 38, an unprecedented recovery rate for the period.

One survivor, Lieutenant Edmund L. Zalinski, thought Mudd deserved clemency for his valiant efforts and petitioned President Andrew Johnson. The letter was signed by 299 officers and soldiers. Johnson signed the pardon on February 2, 1869, and Dr. Mudd returned to his home in Charles County, where he died in January 1883.

In the wake of the many trials and tribulations witnessed by the Mudd family and this historic manor home, there is ample fuel for the paranormal engine. The site was once featured on the television show *Ghost Hunters*, which corroborated many of the supernatural reports.

Wraithlike apparitions, phantom voices and even physical contact have been attested to in the house and on the grounds of the plantation house—now open as a museum. The doctor's wife, Misses "Frankie" Mudd, is the best-known entity haunting the home, but there's also a young child rumored to tug on your pants leg as you tour the building. On the bed where Booth once reclined, a depression in the shape of a man is often seen. Guides, attired in period costume, need to straighten the bed clothes often after visits by the resting spirit. Many have heard the words "I'm not guilty" whispered in their ears.

During one Civil War reenactment, electric candles in the windows flickered off and on by themselves. Visitors have noted sudden bursts of cold in closed rooms and shadowy human profiles reclining on the house's original Civil War–era furnishings.

The vision of Confederate troops marching across the property was reported by one sensitive observer, although why this would be so, I cannot fathom. I've found no historical reference to an encampment there, notwithstanding the aforementioned reenactments.

My research has dispelled another common misconception. The expression "Your name is mud" does not refer to Dr. Mudd, despite

Dr. Mudd's tombstone at Saint Mary's Church, Bryantown, Maryland. *Photo from author's collection.*

popular wisdom and the character Ben Gates (*National Treasure: Book of Secrets*) promoting this inaccuracy. The first printed reference to this saying was in 1823, ten years before Samuel Mudd's birth.

Still, the main questions remain: Was Dr. Mudd guilty or innocent? If guilty, how much of the plot was he privy to? How active was his participation? For over a century, Mudd's family has worked tirelessly to clear their ancestor's name. Could this be the unfinished business at Dr. Mudd's house that's pulling back the curtain separating life and death? Come for a visit soon and decide for yourself.

CRY BABY BRIDGE

Is there any locality in our great country that doesn't have its own version of a "Cry Baby Bridge?" In researching our own, I discovered at least half a dozen others in the country, most located along the Eastern Seaboard.

The guardians of the Southern Maryland version hold a literary double-edged sword. The legend surrounding this tiny bridge in Great Mills, Maryland, has its roots in two historical eras. (The second version can be found with the tales originating during World War II.)

The first fable involves a runaway slave. Remember, Maryland was a slave state—even after the Emancipation Proclamation. The famous document was delivered on January 1, 1863, two years after hostilities began, and it served only to free the slaves in the newly formed Confederacy. This changed the primary focus of the war. No longer was it just an attempt to preserve the Union. Granting freedom for the slaves became the war's legitimate and righteous aim. It also served to keep foreign powers from joining the Rebel cause. Maryland dragged its feet on emancipation for nearly two more years, until November 1, 1864, only months before the Thirteen Amendment was signed.

The young slave woman, Alice, of our Cry Baby Bridge story was owned by a particularly foul slave owner during these in-between years. He had acquired quite a few slaves over the years; modern DNA tests would confirm that he fathered many of them.

The perversions that the man subjected Alice to eventually impregnated her. During the following months, as her belly swelled, the depraved master left her alone. Although that was a blessing, after her little one's birth, Alice knew it was a matter of time before he summoned her back to his bed. Alice's spirit was ripped in two—not only was her torture about to begin anew, but also her dear child would be raised a slave. She saw no future for herself or her progeny, so she devised a plan.

The following week, Alice was informed that her master was waiting for her in the bedroom down the hall from the one he shared with his wife. Alice crept to his room with a small cast-iron saucepan held behind her back. After a rap at the door, she entered to find him stretched out on the bed. She stepped toward him. When his hand reached for her, she swung the pan and whacked him on the side of his bald head.

Cry Baby Creek East by the bridge. *Photo from author's collection.*

The man's head flopped on his pillow as blood oozed from his ears and nostrils. Alice knew she'd struck too hard. She ran down to the far side of the house, snatched up her child and fled through the swampy woods surrounding the tobacco farm.

It was early the next morning before the slave owner's wife noticed his absence and searched the house. On discovering the fate of the pestilence that she called a husband, a posse was assembled. A local raccoon hunter brought his Redbone hounds to join in the search through the swamp.

They captured Alice near the wooden plank bridge on the far edge of the plantation. They ripped the squealing baby boy from her arms and slipped a noose around her neck and hanged her from a large maple tree. Alice's child rolled down the embankment to drown in the shallow water of the creek and washed downstream in the current. Some of the residents of the area claim the little one's cries are still heard on windless nights. (Author's note: a second version of this story places its origin on St. John's Road in Hollywood, Maryland.)

ST. MARY'S OF BRYANTOWN

St. Mary's Catholic Church of Bryantown was organized in 1793 and became a separate parish in 1851. Land was initially donated in 1743 from a section of the original Boarman's Manor. The stated intent was for the construction of a "log cabin church" on the property to serve the community. In 1845, a brick church was constructed and rebuilt in 1963 after fire gutted the building.

The School Sisters of Notre Dame arrived in 1915 and founded two schools on the property, a separate "colored" school and a "white" school. A senior high school and a boarding school were added in 1921. The boarding school functioned until 1931, while the high school kept its doors open until 1967.

The federally mandated desegregation of the early 1960s brought the "colored school" to a close, and demolition was completed by the late sixties. Thirty years later, a beautiful memorial was erected to commemorate the students who'd attended there. In 1967, the school opened as a new elementary school for all children.

So, what supernatural delights await us at St. Mary's Church? There are those who say the very air around the old convent raises the hair on the back of their necks. Perhaps it is a stern-faced nun determined to instill obedience in her rebellious charges? Or should we take a jaunt outside to the cemetery that surrounds the church? The graves date back to the colonial period, many undocumented after a 1963 fire destroyed cemetery records. One can hardly doubt that some of the deceased, over all of those years, had unfinished business. Or perhaps they met untimely or violent deaths?

One frequent visitor and worker at the parish has stories to tell. Once, all alone, and putting the finishing touches on Christmas wreaths for the holiday decor, she heard a radio playing. She assumed someone left it playing by mistake. But perhaps someone else was there? Leaving the old science lab, she determined that the sound was emanating from upstairs. One can only imagine the trepidation at each step up those stairs: all alone in an old building on a cold wintry night, hearing noises where there should be none.

Step by creaking step she ascended the wooden steps until she got halfway up to the second floor. Something gave her pause there, when a very distinct voice was heard.

"Get out! You aren't supposed to be here."

"Yes I am. Who is this?," our brave volunteer responded. The air around the stairway became very cold.

Again the spectral voice said, "Get out!"

That was enough. There was no question in her mind about what she'd just experienced, and she left the building (and the grounds) posthaste. As is often the case with stories regarding the unknown or unexplained, when she shared her experience with someone, it was laughed off. So, she managed to forget about it over the next few years…until she decided to share it again. She was upstairs for a meeting in the same building. It may be that her audience seemed more receptive, or that she wanted to lighten the mood. But on an impulse at the conclusion of her tale, she said, "If you are here tonight, let us know."

No sooner were the words spoken than the telephone on the wall rang. The meeting attendees looked back and forth at one another, and a brave soul snatched up the phone—but there was only static on the other end.

The old rectory building is now used for classrooms and offices, but it once housed the School Sisters of Notre Dame. Their bedrooms were upstairs.

Several people have reported leaving the school building and feeling someone (or something) staring out of the upstairs window. Random lights are found turned on when people swear they turned them off. The school building seems peaceful, though, if there are any "visitors from the beyond." The rectory building is the place many suggest we steer clear of—there's said to be a strong presence there.

St. Mary's Church, Bryantown, Maryland. *Photo from author's collection.*

So, what is the source of these haunts? Should we assume the good sisters spent so much time and lavished so much love at this site that they're unable to let it go or to move on to their eternal reward? But nuns are known as disciplinarians. They wouldn't take an intrusion into their spaces lightly. That would seem the obvious answer regarding the old rectory building. But what about the rest of the property? The answer may reside under one particular grave marker. For the most famous resident of the marble field is none other than Dr. Samuel Mudd, the man who set John Wilkes Booth's leg so many years ago. Is the good doctor still distraught over his ill treatment by the law and by how history remembered him? Or has Booth sought out his one-time physician to cure his spiritual ailments?

As this is the resting place of Dr. Mudd and also the church where Mudd and Booth first met, the grounds are included in the state-sponsored "Booth's Escape Scenic Byway." Many sites along this trail are reported to be haunted.

CROSS MANOR

A famous St. Mary's County ghost story is related to another notable location in this book, Rooke's Lodge, although the actual event occurred at Cross Manor. The manor was established by Thomas Cornwallis in 1633, likely awarded for services rendered to the colonial government as a politician, administrator and captain in the colony's militia. Cornwallis was not the first-born son and so couldn't hope to inherit his father's holdings in England. His family was Roman Catholic and, therefore, pariahs in England. These two circumstances made the thought of a colony in the New World welcoming England's Catholics especially appealing.

At the time of the tragedies that gave rise to our ghost stories, however, Cross Manor was owned by Dr. Caleb Jones. He'd purchased Rooke's Lodge for his son, Captain Randolph Jones, and his wife to reside in. However, it wasn't meant to be.

The Cross Manor site, especially while under the ownership of Dr. Jones, was no stranger to tragedy. There was a shipwreck here in November 1864 involving the gunboat USS *Tulip*. The *Tulip* was assigned to the Potomac flotilla during the Civil War, and its normal docking place was at Jones' Wharf on Cross Manor. It's said that Captain Randolph Jones was very friendly with the Northern troops, much to the annoyance of his fellow Southern

Marylanders. The *Tulip* left that day on its way to the Washington Navy Yard for boiler repairs. Just past Ragged Point, Virginia, the boilers exploded and blew gaping holes in the gunboat. Men grabbed what they could to keep them afloat as the ship sank. An hour later, the *Hudson* spotted the wreckage and searched the floating debris. Of the sixty-nine crew members, only ten survivors were pulled from the waters. Of those ten, two died as a result of their injuries. The U.S. government erected a monument to the men who died that day. With the reported sights and sounds associated with this site, it would appear these men aren't ready to accept their untimely fate.

The story of the second wreck associated with Cross Manor began on October 1878. Mrs. Randolph Jones left Cross Manor to travel by the steamboat *Express* to Baltimore. According to legend, it was her intent on this journey to procure furniture to set up housekeeping at Rooke's Lodge. On the return trip, she'd disembark at Jones' Wharf on Cross Manor (later called Grayson's Wharf), a popular drop-off point in Southern Maryland. On October 22, the *Express* was caught in a hurricane on the Chesapeake Bay near Point Lookout. There were nine passengers and twenty-two crew members on board.

According to the report in the *Baltimore Gazette*, "as far as James' Point weather was rough and the steamer was pitching badly, but no alarm was felt. After passing that point, the wind increased in velocity to a frightful extent and the steamer finally became unmanageable and rolled in the trough of the sea….Again and again the fierce waves swept over the ill-fated steamer, and the captain abandoned all hope."

The captain is said to have found his two lady passengers, Mary A. Bacon and Mrs. Captain Randolph Jones—both of St. Mary's County. He helped adjust their life preservers and placed them at the stern of the vessel with the admonition that the ship was about to be torn to pieces. He promised to render aid if at all possible.

The heavy waves divested the ship of most of its crew and passengers even before the steamer fell apart in the night. Some of the crew survived until rescue arrived by clinging to floating debris, but of the thirty-one persons on board, only nine crew members were saved. None of the passengers survived.

Mrs. Jones drowned, and her body was found on the eastern shore of the bay some time later, but death, it seems, did not end her adventure of that fateful night.

Two versions exist as to the happenings at Cross Manor as they waited for the return of Randolph's wife. It's both said that he was entertaining guests and that he was having a small gathering with friends. I suppose it's a moot point, but the rest of the story is as it's been passed down by Captain Jones himself.

As they waited for the *Express* to arrive at the pier, the storm raged around them. At one point, they heard a knock at the front door. As it was the time the *Express* was expected, Caleb Jones looked out of the window and saw his son's wife standing at the door. Rushing to the door to get the young woman out of the weather, they threw the door open wide…but no one was there.

I'm sure little sleep was had that night at Cross Manor as they waited for the steamboat or news of the same—ever hoping the ship waited in port instead of tempting the storm waters. The next day, Captain Jones received news of the ship's sinking and the death of his beloved. He and his father both swore the timing of the ship's demise paralleled the vision of his wife at their door.

Captain Jones never did live at Rooke's Lodge, and the dreams he shared with his wife died with her. In 1893, the property was purchased by Bevins Morris as part of a larger farm known as Jutland. The Rooke's Lodge portion was inherited by his daughter Edith Morris Abell and remains in the family until this day.

Cross Manor has also been known as the Manor of Cornwallis's Cross. It is a privately owned property and is listed in the National Register of Historic Places for Maryland.

6

WORLD WAR I

A WORLD DIVIDED

The United States declared war on Germany in April 1917. Southern Maryland, along with the rest of the state, sent many sons and daughters to support the war effort. African American men and women of Maryland, only a generation away from enslavement, participated to the tune of over eleven thousand troops sent to serve during the period.

In July 1917, the navy assumed control of a small maritime organization from Maryland's State Conservation Commission that was dubbed, appropriately, the "Oyster Navy."

Through the war years, more than sixty-two thousand Marylanders served in the war. Of those, nearly two thousand lost their lives. By the end of the war, the country had enough of sacrificing its sons and daughters in foreign wars. Eyes and hearts turned inward.

DRUM POINT LIGHTHOUSE

The Drum Point Lighthouse was built in 1883 to safeguard passage of mariners into the Patuxent River from the Chesapeake Bay. The light served the sailors well over the years, with many updates along the way, converting to electricity in 1944 and becoming fully automated only sixteen years later (1960). In 1962, the light was replaced initially by a lighted buoy, and still later a fixed offshore light was installed. The lighthouse remained on the point for many years, abandoned.

The Calvert County Historical Society realized the historical significance of the lighthouse and made many attempts to acquire the lighthouse property, to no avail. Finally, in 1974, it did gain possession—of the building. The federal government retained the land on which it sat. The years of neglect and vandalism didn't do the building any good, and the decision was made to cut the light from the ground. It then rode a barge to its current location at the Calvert Marine Museum in Solomons, Maryland. Grants and donations made a complete restoration possible. A rededication ceremony was held to officially open the lighthouse as an exhibit in 1978.

Staff members of the Calvert Marine Museum are no strangers to the eerie phenomena at this reportedly haunted lighthouse. Many have stated that items are moved about in the interior of the lighthouse. Cut flowers are tossed from their vases and scattered across the floor. Distinct footsteps have been heard moving up and down the stairs—when no visitors were present.

One report states that a lighthouse keeper's hat has been moved around. (Perhaps he came back for a visit and didn't want the sun in his face?) Many have reported seeing a spectral brunette woman pacing the lighthouse and

Drum Point Lighthouse in its current location at Calvert Marine Museum. *Photo from author's collection.*

staring across the river. Is she waiting for her beloved to return? Or is she helping some long-ago lighthouse keeper in his duties?

During my recent visit there, the lighthouse was deserted. The museum itself was closed for renovations, and I'm looking forward to its reopening. While I was there, I wandered around the grounds and especially the lighthouse. I had my recorder in hand, and when I listened to it later, there was a "clicking" sound that wasn't heard while at the site. When I played it again at home, my wife immediately came to the same conclusion as I had—it sounded like Morse code.

Alfred Vail and Samuel Morse introduced their telegraph and code in May 1844. A variant of the system was used in some lighthouses, the flash's duration indicating dots and dashes. It's not much of a stretch to assume any professional lighthouse keeper would know the Morse alphabet. The volume of the tapping on my recording, however, fluctuated, to the point that it was impossible to get a clear read on the quantity and sequence of dots and dashes to translate, if one assumed it was indeed a coded message from the beyond. Whether you're a ghost hunter or just mildly curious, a believer or a skeptic, Solomons Island is a renowned tourist stop. If you find yourself in the area, the Calvert Marine Museum is a must-see.

On a side note, the complete logbooks from the entire period that the lighthouse was manned were preserved and filed at the National Archives. They provide an accurate view of a keeper's daily life.

GHOST FLEET OF MALLOWS BAY

The Mallows Bay story begins when the United States entered World War I. We had plenty of warships, learning that much from previous wars, but transport vessels were in short supply. That began a huge shipbuilding enterprise, with a standing order (and an eighteen-month deadline) for one thousand steamships.

With little time, the shipbuilders used wood in lieu of steel whenever possible, a material reserved for combat vessels, which technically these ships were not. When the Germans surrendered in November 1918, none of these newly commissioned vessels had yet crossed the Atlantic.

The U.S. Navy had no further use for the vessels, and the ships and shipyard were abandoned. The vessels were temporarily stored in harbor on the James River—290 leaky and unwanted ships. Storage wasn't cheap, and something needed to be done to alleviate the expense.

Thus began the first, but not the last, attempt at salvage/scrap in the following years. The ships were moved to Widewater, Virginia, an approved site for the salvage endeavor. Local watermen balked at the scheme and protested vehemently, and operations were halted.

Western Marine and Salvage purchased 566 acres opposite Widewater in Mallows Bay on the Maryland shoreline of the Potomac. The company moved the hulks there and torched the ships.

Years later, after Western Marine went bankrupt and World War II loomed on the horizon, Bethlehem Steel had a go at the salvage effort. Spending nearly $500,000 in the effort, it recouped minimal return on its investment.

Researchers at Mallows Bay have discovered eighty-eight wooden ships left over from the original U.S. order, twelve barges, a Revolutionary War–era longboat, some eighteenth-century schooners and multiple abandoned workboats. The "Ghost Fleet" is situated on the tidal Potomac in Charles County, Maryland. The small bay holds the largest collection of shipwrecks in the Western Hemisphere. The original ships measure up to three hundred feet long, and their remains "rise" out of the water at low

One of the ships in the Ghost Fleet of Mallows Bay. *Compliments of Tourism Department of Recreation, Parks & Tourism of Charles County.*

tide, their skeletons an eerie sight on a foggy morning—thus the nickname the "Ghost Fleet of Mallows Bay."

Floating between the hulks in a small kayak (Mallows Bay is a popular destination for kayakers such as the author), the eerie feeling cannot be ignored—even the most skeptical people feel the hairs raise on their necks and shivers run down their spines.

The appearance of the ghost ships isn't the only reason for these feelings. Several people have been killed when their boats flipped after getting caught in the thick metal cables used as mooring lines.

As recently as the 1970s, a young woman committed suicide here. She drove down to the point, set down her shoes and purse on the sand and walked into the river to her death.

There's no denying that Mallows Bay is a scary place, even without the knowledge of people dying here.

COVE POINT LIGHTHOUSE

The lighthouse that originally stood guarding the water off Cove Point was initially intended to be built at Cedar Point to the south. However, Congress received numerous petitions from sailors and watermen in the area prioritizing the requirement for a lighthouse at Cove Point for ships entering the Patuxent River. The squeaky wheel gets the grease, and the lighthouse contract for Cove Point was awarded to John Donahoo, a very prolific lighthouse builder in the area.

The Cove Point Lighthouse was built in 1828 and a second story was added in 1883. It stood thirty-six feet tall, built of masonry with a winding staircase that ascended to the original lantern. Many improvements were made over the years until the old building was completely renovated in 1986 with the addition of a lamp changer, a fog detector and a computer connecting it to the mainland. These improvements rendered the lighthouse keeper's position obsolete.

The lighthouse station was transferred to Calvert County from the Coast Guard in October 2000. The Calvert Marine Museum now provides access to the public even as the facility remains an active aid to navigation. The Calvert Marine Museum Society updated the keeper's quarters into two weekly vacation rentals. Each side has three bedrooms, two and a half baths, a living room and a kitchen.

Prior to the United States entering World War I in April 1917, tensions were already high in Southern Maryland and the rest of the country. Our involvement seemed imminent. One month before, on March 15, the seventy-two-year-old lighthouse keeper, Richard S. Daniels, died of a heart attack while conversing with the captain of the *Maple*. The ship was on its appointed rounds to maintain and support the lighthouse.

It seems that old lighthouses naturally draw paranormal phenomena. Is there a lighthouse anywhere that doesn't boast a ghost or two? I'm sure that Cove Point is no exception, and as it is the only operational lighthouse in Maryland (and remains open to the public), perhaps you, too, will be lucky enough to hear Mr. Daniels making his daily rounds.

7

WORLD WAR II

THE WAR TO END ALL WARS

M any changes came to Southern Maryland in the war years. The beginning of the 1940s saw the arrival of two very different communities: the Amish and the Old Order Mennonites established their farms; and on April 1, 1943, Patuxent River Naval Air Station was commissioned. It's hard to imagine more dissimilar groups of "settlers."

During the World War II years, Southern Marylanders came to the nation's defense once again. Saint Mary's County alone had 1,442 people join the military ranks, an impressive number, representing nearly 10 percent of the county's total population in 1940.

Many Southern Marylanders never returned. As late as 2012, the family of one man, Captain Walter Francis Duke of Leonardtown, was informed his body might have been found. The captain was shot down in combat over the Burmese jungles in 1944. The *Baltimore Sun* called him "Maryland's leading air ace of World War II."

Across the Patuxent in Calvert County, the USN housed the Naval Mine Warfare Test Station, Naval Amphibious Training Base, Mine Warfare Experimental Station and Naval Dispensary on Solomon's Island. More than sixty thousand troops trained at these facilities in the World War II years.

The postwar years began with prosperity for Marylanders and most Americans. It was the era of scientific discovery as well as the age of the atomic bomb. A long period of national paranoia followed as the Cold War began—the great divide between communism and capitalism.

CRY BABY BRIDGE (VERSION 2)

Cry Baby Bridge West. *Photo from author's collection.*

The oldest reference to paranormal activity for this innocuous-looking bridge was listed under the stories from the Civil War. The second contender for the source of the haunting of the Cry Baby Bridge phenomena (or perhaps the second haunting?) occurs immediately after World War II. The tale is a basic one, but it has spanned the years with many retellings and versions.

The most widely accepted version is that a soldier is on his way home from his lengthy stint overseas, a duty that began shortly after his wedding day. His beautiful young wife waits for him at home—a wife and an infant son he's never met.

The man is so excited; it's been forever since he's so much as heard his bride's sweet voice. He convinces his driver to pull over at a phone booth ten miles from his home. He calls his beloved with the news that he's on his way—almost there, in fact!

The wife is overwhelmed and paces the floor. She wanders back and forth between the two windows facing the street, looking for the flash of lights signaling her husband's return. Finally, she wraps her infant son in a bundle of blankets and runs from the house, determined not to waste a single moment with her man—she'd meet up with him on the road.

The husband's driver floors the vehicle, egged on by the impatient man in the passenger's seat. On the last turn before the soldier's house, the headlights flash on the figure of a woman in the road. The driver slams on the brakes, fishtailing in the narrow road, but it's too late. The sickening thump of metal meeting flesh.

The men jump from the vehicle to discover the soldier's wife crushed in the road. The child whom she'd clung to so tightly had been tossed from her arms and now lay broken on the rocks below. The husband's screams were silenced over time, but the wails of the infant remain.

This is truly a dark tale, but it may reflect the fatalism of the period. By the way, an even darker version of the story says the husband was cuckolded during his absence. He returned home to find a new baby—too young to have sprouted from his loins—and he killed his wife and the child. It must be the romantic in me, but I'll stick with the first version.

Patuxent River NAWC/AD

Pearl Harbor caught the nation unawares on December 7, 1941. For the country, it was "a date which will live in infamy," and it was no different in Southern Maryland. For some residents, though, it struck home on a very personal level.

On December 13, 1941, a federal marshal traveled to Saint Mary's County, Maryland, to the long-established towns on Cedar Point. He was tacking eviction notice signs to the doors of all residents' homes with explicit orders to vacate the property by April 17, 1942. The entire point was declared condemned and taken over by the authority established under eminent domain. Farms and homes were sold for a fraction of their actual value. The more affluent property owners took the government to court and were given substantially more. Poorer residents couldn't afford the luxury of hiring lawyers to pursue legal relief.

Many of the descendants of these displaced residents of Jarboesville, Pearson, Susquehanna, Mattapany and Fordstown state that their ancestors never recovered from this forced evacuation. It was difficult losing family land that had been held since the mid-1600s and seeing homes and barns bulldozed to the ground. After the news of the U.S. Navy moving into the area, land prices soared. Few could establish holdings similar to what they'd had before. Many moved away from the area entirely.

The establishment of the bases in the 1940s brought prosperity to the region, and its impact on the area's culture is equally apparent. The population of Saint Mary's County, Maryland, in 1940 was 14,626. In ten years, it swelled to 29,111. This dramatic doubling of the population changed the rural character of the land, and the process nearly repeated itself between 1980 and 2010 (59,895 to 105,764 residents), according to U.S. Census reports.

Few residents today would argue the intrinsic value of the naval bases along Southern Maryland's shores. The test programs and test-pilot school contribute substantially to both our national defense and our local economy. A poor rural community has developed into a bastion of modernity and cutting-edge technology. Dirt trails morphed into multi-lane roads, and employment opportunities bloomed. But it was at a heavy cost to the prior owners of the properties. Their lives and livelihoods were ripped from them as swiftly as a rug pulled out from under their feet. Small wonder, then, that many of the banished have returned—even if not in this life.

I've personally had the hair stand up on my neck while standing at the Pearson memorial picnic spot. Many campers in the area have reported ghostly apparitions through the trees. A spectral lady who makes no sound suddenly appears in the mists off the river. She is the ghost who is reported most often. Perhaps she's one of the displaced who has returned to her ancestral home? Or is she one of those buried here whose burial site was plowed under? Maybe our lady once called Mattapany-Sewall manor her home? It was once occupied by Charles Calvert, the Third Baron of Baltimore. He lived there from 1666 to 1684. It was also the site of the 1689 battle that overthrew the government of Maryland (the Protestant Revolution). Perhaps our ghostly lady was caught in the crossfire?

One of the regularly reported hauntings is that of Building 409, the location of the Command Duty Office. The *Tester* (Patuxent River's USN-sanctioned newspaper) reported the experiences of several sailors performing the night duty there. They reported the sounds of chairs rolling across the second-story floors after the area was locked up for the night. Footsteps and voices were heard when the building was otherwise deserted. Doorknobs were jingled as if someone wanted access to a locked room. They've claimed an eerie feeling halfway up the stairs when investigating—a strong sense of not being alone. Once, a "wet floor" sign propped itself open after having been folded up and put away. Was it just a mischievous sailor trying to spook his companion? Or was it something more? Something otherworldly?

It's not only our men and women in uniform who draw the attention of the wayward spirits at Patuxent River, however. I was recently privileged to meet with a lady whose formative years were spent in base housing and grew up running through the fields and woods of this beautiful naval installation.

Like most children, her peers shared stories of haunts and fearful tales. Given the timeline of occupation of this desirable piece of property and the many lives lived and lost on its fertile shores, there's little wonder why the land has absorbed the "vibes" of the past. And it was inevitable that the current residents might have their own stories to tell.

A scary playground, seemingly forgotten, was described to me as looking like a horror story location, complete with creaky teeter-totters, rusted swings and warped slides. Once, when returning home through the woods, they heard steps approaching through the leaves. At first, they waited, thinking it to be a deer, but as it continued in a straight line toward them, their concern grew. They started to walk away, slowly at first, but faster as the steps continued matching their speed. By the time they cleared the woods, their pace would have made an Olympic sprinter proud. They gasped for air, collecting themselves before they went back into their homes. Was it a man or a beast that spooked them that day? Or some other…thing?

I was told that the feeling of being watched was felt often by the band of friends. Overactive imaginations, some might say. There was plenty to fertilize young imaginations there, including a story about the murdered mother and child from the area. Rumors floated about Carpenter Park housing being built over a Native American burial site. One building that they encountered they nicknamed the "Powerhouse," as it looked like a mechanical monstrosity. It was in an isolated area of the base and was what one might imagine finding in a psychopath's basement at the intended victim's moment of terror. It had doors locked shut with heavy chains. A hole where the doorknob once was allowed inquisitive peeks into the darkened room. My spectral informant said they thought they saw movements inside on occasions but suspected that this at least might be imagination at work, though the grapevine held that men had gone there to work and were never heard from again.

I found the lady who shared these stories with me to be extremely grounded and forthright. Still, skeptics might explain them away as imaginative musings by credulous children. But there were plenty of undeniable terrors there as well. There was a vacant and locked building where windows kept shattering, the glass pushed outward. An apartment building raised the hairs on their necks when they passed by and every week or so had police tape over a different doorway. As nothing was reported, what was going on there? While on their frequent jaunts, the plucky group of young people discovered what appeared to be desecrated graves, or at least apparently old and broken tombstones, perhaps victims of time rather than human hands. The old theater (prior to renovation) held its own terrors. A disembodied voice by one person's side said, "Shhh," when nobody was there. A witness in the restroom, behind a locked stall, saw the lock slowly turn from the outside—again, nobody was there.

Enjoying all of these tales as I did, I was still unprepared and enthralled by my source's descriptions of "the kids." She wasn't sure exactly when they made their first appearance in her home on Carpenter Park, but they really got the family's attention after they performed a simple household chore. For some time, odd occurrences were happening in the new home. Television channels changed on their own, and lights cut on and off by themselves. Usually, these phenomena were accompanied by the sound of young people giggling. This was witnessed by numerous visitors to the home. One morning, the mother, following her normal routine, went back to the bedroom to make up the bed. To her surprise (and horror), she found the bed already made. She was positive she'd not done so, and it appeared to have been accomplished by inept hands. This reoccurred several times over the years; after the first time, little notice was taken. Other than the inherent fear of the unknown, the family felt no real threat from the entities. The "kids" were just being mischievous, leg-pulling scallywags. It's interesting to note that when the activity became too much of a nuisance, the residents could order them to stop. And they would.

Although the family grew accustomed to the pranks played by the "kids," I'm sure there was some degree of relief when they moved off the base to a new home. If so, the relief was short lived, as they soon discovered that the kids had followed them. All the earlier irritations began anew. Lights cut on and off, television channels changed, steps were heard across the floor upstairs when that floor was empty and there was the feeling that someone stood beside you, when no corporeal body was to be seen. In fact, if anything, the ghostlike happenings increased.

One morning, the mother walked into the living room, having heard voices, only to find nobody there. She questioned her daughter whether she'd been watching television, but she had not. The mother heard two people discussing an upcoming cotillion where a Sir Randolph would also be in attendance—not a likely conversation for the time. The title "Sir Randolph" presents two possible candidates. Sir Richard Randolph of Northamptonshire, England, was the brother of Captain Henry Randolph of Virginia. Perhaps he made the journey across the sea to visit with his brother? A cotillion was an event they'd surely not wish to miss. A more likely candidate, however, is Sir John Randolph (1693–1737) of Williamsburg, Virginia. He was a member of Virginia's House of Burgesses. His status, wealth and knighthood would certainly have turned the young ladies' eyes.

The kids seemed to make themselves comfortable in the new home and are still present to this day. Many visitors have reported interactions with them over the years. House sitters have declined to return, and an in-law refused to ever stay overnight there again.

When our witness returned home as a young woman (after her own service in the military), she had additional experiences. One morning, as she was trying to go back to sleep, she heard her mother walk in, circle her bed and then leave…and found out later that it wasn't her mother at all. Shortly after, she was alone and felt someone blow forcibly at her ear, pushing her hair into the air. Her mother has also reported having her hair "played with."

After all these years, their response to most contacts with the phantom adolescents is, "Oh, well, it's just the 'kids.'"

PINEY POINT LIGHTHOUSE

Piney Point Lighthouse is another creation of the famed lighthouse builder John Donahoo. He utilized the time-proven design of a conical stone tower. This lighthouse scaled the heights at thirty-five feet and included a lighthouse keeper's quarters built separate from the tower. In 1836, the design was completed and the light flickered to life for the first time.

The lighthouse was located fourteen miles north of the Potomac's confluence with the Chesapeake Bay. Its location made it an ideal getaway from the stresses of city life, and it soon became known as the "President's light house." Teddy Roosevelt, Franklin Pierce and James Monroe were all known to have relaxed in the shade of the tower and fished the waters of the Potomac here.

Sadly, the lighthouse was decommissioned in 1964, but its saga continues. Taken over by Saint Mary's County Recreation and Parks in 1990, it is now open to the public. Since its opening, it's been turned into a veritable cornucopia for curious mariners, military fans, lighthouse lovers and history aficionados. During World War II, a German U-boat, called a Black Panther, was captured and eventually towed to Piney Point to be sunk. The *U-1105* submarine now serves as Maryland's first historic shipwreck dive preserve.

Over the years, many possible hauntings have been reported, including by construction workers repairing the old structures. They recounted hearing disembodied voices that frequently distracted their efforts. Others have described the same, and a paranormal unit called the D.C. Hauntings Paranormal Group investigated. Oddly, it never released its findings, and I fear it is now defunct. I can find no current references to the group. Did its members hear Germanic orders barked at crewmen they couldn't see? It's said that disembodied spirits return to the scene of their greatest triumphs, especially if their later years were lived in shame. Is there then a more likely candidate than that engendered by the saga of the U-boat and its sailors? Perhaps the investigators recorded the cries of wrecked seamen from the days before the lighthouse safely lit their way? Or maybe they heard nothing at all…

During my visit to the lighthouse, I heard no spectral voices, but I will confess to feeling "odd," especially as I walked around the base of the keeper's house. My recorder picked up no verifiable EVPs, but there were sounds I could not readily identify. The strange feeling I attribute to being alone in the presence of history, a place where many have lived, loved, labored and died.

Piney Point Lighthouse. *Photo from author's collection.*

The surrounding park and museum boast many activities to draw your interest—notwithstanding the ghostly elements. You can climb the oldest lighthouse on the Potomac, see the many restored historic boats and learn some maritime history in the museum. Offshore, the sunken World War II–era *U-1105* (U-boat) is a Historic Shipwreck Dive Preserve. Stop by and take a walk on the beach, launch your kayak or bring a picnic lunch. Even though the ghosts seldom pester a daytime visitor, keep an eye out…just in case.

8

MODERN ERA

THE BIRTH OF SCIENTIFIC REASON?

One thing became apparent to me as I perused my notes and research to format these stories in sequential order. The further I've gone back in time, the more reports can be found of hauntings and the birth of paranormal activities. I've no doubt this is largely attributable to the birth of "scientific reasoning," but the legends are so prevalent in Southern Maryland, I doubt there's a farm, a road, a creek or an old farmhouse that doesn't have at least one haunt associated with it.

Perhaps the repetition from one generation to the next contributes to a legend's validation? Or do tragic events and circumstances need time to ferment before they make themselves known in the areas where they occurred? Unfinished business? Won't we all have that someday…no matter how well we plan?

In the here and now, we have all the requisite ingredients for a haunt or two. There's been tragedy on our shores and waterways for as long as men have walked our woods and drifted the creeks and rivers. In this bountiful land of milk and honey (and stuffed ham and crab cakes), folks have been (and continue to be) killed, tortured, abused, cheated and maligned. And so it goes…

From the battles between pre-Columbian native groups, who've left their bones in our fertile soils, to the horrors of the Oyster Wars, when the rivers tasted blood, again.

We've come this far, let's go there together:

F/A-18 in U.S. Navy photo. *Photographer's Mate Third-Class Jayme Pastoric.*

THE OYSTER WARS

Most sources give the dates of the "Oyster Wars" as beginning in 1865 and ending in 1962, when President John F. Kennedy signed the Potomac Fisheries Bill establishing a bistate commission to oversee the Potomac River. Even before this time, however, a violent and competitive friction existed on the Potomac and Chesapeake waterways. It manifested itself over three waves of tragedy and bloodied Southern Maryland's waters.

Both Maryland and Virginia claimed ownership of the Potomac, having legal documentation tracing back to grants from the Crown. In the Compact of 1785, Virginia agreed that Maryland's claim was the strongest and conceded, while retaining fishing rights and free access to the Potomac. The peace proved to be fragile when the oyster beds shrunk from overharvesting and Maryland imposed harvesting restrictions. Bloody battles ensued.

Two state factions, led by James Madison (Virginia) and Samuel Chase (Maryland), agreed to meet and air their dispute in Annapolis in 1786. When few delegates showed up, they rescheduled the meeting for May in Philadelphia.

Retired Oyster "Buy Boat" on display at Calvert Marine Museum. *Photo from author's collection.*

The federal government, then restrained by the Articles of Confederation, could not raise an army for defense, coin money or regulate interstate commerce. The meeting between the aggrieved states coalesced into the Constitutional Convention. The lowly oyster lit a spark that lead to a new government!

After the Civil War, oyster prices zoomed even as the oyster beds in Long Island Sound and Cape Cod were depleted. To protect its interests and waterways, Maryland added a requirement for an annual permit, limited to residents. Despite this, oyster pirates descended from the north on the bay and the Potomac with their large dredging boats (dredging was outlawed here in 1830). In response, Maryland chartered the "Oyster Navy" with fifty men in 1868 to end the poaching.

Once their common enemy was defeated, the neighboring states returned to their feuding. Small, fast boats, equipped with dual engines, were employed to outrun the police and gave rise to their nickname—the Mosquito Fleet.

The confrontations with the police came to a head on April 17, 1959. In the wee hours of the morning, Berkeley Muse met up with his friend Harvey

King in a pool hall in Colonial Beach, Virginia. King, a known poacher, stated his intention to dredge oysters before the new dawn illuminated his illegal activities. Berkeley went along with his friend and another man, John Griffith, when King's boat left the dock around 3:00 a.m.

Two police boats patrolled the Potomac in the darkness: the *Honga River* and the *McKeldin*—repurposed PT boats. When the fog lifted, King spotted the *Honga River* barreling toward them and fired up his boat's two seventy-five-horsepower outboards. King's boat pulled away from the slower police boat. The *Honga River* threw an engine bearing in the chase and fired on the smaller boat in what the officers aboard described as "warning shots." The *McKeldin* approached from the opposite direction, forcing King to swerve back toward the *Honga River*—even as it continued its barrage. Berkeley Muse yelled, "I'm hit" and slumped over the boat's culling board. The firing continued, and King was hit in the leg. Rushing to shore, Muse died before the ambulance arrived.

Public outcry after the incident lead to the disarming of the police force and eventually to Kennedy's Potomac Fisheries Commission. These actions effectively ended the bloody Oyster Wars.

Shell heap of Southern Maryland's favorite bivalve. *Photo from author's collection.*

Over the years spanning two centuries, small arms and cannon fire were employed to protect state and private interests. It's estimated that hundreds of watermen from both shores met their demise chasing their livelihoods. No wonder then that so many modern-day watermen, as tough and weather-hardened as can be, report shivers running down their backs in certain places on the creeks and rivers. It's easy to believe in the seldom-reported spectral voices that whisper, "Don't shoot," "Pull anchor" and "I'm killed."

ADAM'S TAP-HOUSE & GRILLE

Adam's Ribs restaurant is known not only for its mouth-watering barbeque delights. Frequent customers of the establishment as well as longtime servers are very familiar with the tale of (if not the experience of) its resident ghost.

The site of this business has been around for a while. In fact, its origin is a log cabin built in the mid-1950s. In the 1970s, Douglas and Nancy Schwab opened it as the Rustic Farm Restaurant and resided in the home behind the inn.

On March 6, 1980, Douglas Schwab reached behind the cash register and, in front of witnesses, retrieved his revolver. When he saw that he was being observed, he told them there was "trouble in the back" and proceeded out of the back door toward where his home was situated.

In a short period of time, he returned to the restaurant and confessed that he'd just shot his wife, Nancy. Police arrived on the scene moments later and arrested Douglas Schwab. They discovered his wife dead, having sustained a gunshot wound to the head. The court convicted Douglas, and he was sentenced to twenty years in jail.

Over the years, the establishment has been called the Rustic Farm Restaurant, the Cabin Inn, Adam's Ribs and, finally, today, Adam's Tap-house & Grille. The names have changed, but the haunted happenings have continued. Employees and customers alike report television sets cutting on and off of their own accord. This is especially noted around closing time. Patrons have reported seeing a spectral apparition that they assume is Nancy Schwab's ghost. Many also claim a feeling of being watched or not alone.

Paranormal investigators arrived at the restaurant in March 2003. Orb pictures were taken—despite camera malfunctions—and several unidentified sounds were heard, but the investigators stated in their report that they could not prove or disprove any paranormal activity.

The restaurant is known for its exceptional ribs, as the name indicates, but its pulled meats and wings are also recommended. If you go there, and a plate is dropped or a drink is spilled, don't be surprised when your wait staff tells you, "Nancy did it."

CHOPTICON HIGH SCHOOL

Chopticon High School was built as a replacement for Margaret Brent High School (now a middle school) in Mechanicsville, Maryland. The small town of Morganza, Maryland, saw this new high school open its doors to students in 1965. I lived across the woods from the school at the time (and I'm still within the sound of its marching band), so I'm familiar with the events that lead to the supposed paranormal activity.

The instigator of this haunting is the convicted murderer Lester Broome. In August 1983, Broome was a teenager (eighteen) working as a summer custodian at the school. Beverly Jo Heater was a well-loved teacher at the school. It's said that she was popular among the students as well as with the rest of the faculty. However, the police report indicates that Broome hated Heater, although the source of his loathing is unknown. Perhaps a bad grade he'd received or… well, who knows what drives someone to commit such a deed?

On one bright August afternoon, Heater was at the school, like many teachers then and now, working whatever hours were necessary for the good of her students. One can only surmise that Broome saw her arrival as a prime opportunity to act on his hate. Broome attacked the teacher and dragged her down the hall to the men's bathroom, where he raped her and stabbed her to death. I was working in my yard when I heard the initial news reports on the radio. It felt like the end of an era. It wasn't as if nothing evil had ever occurred here in the past (just read some of the other accounts listed herein), but the depths of this malevolence, and the degree of violence, was stunning in our small rural community. Then and now, I feel for this poor soul and her family that was left behind.

I cannot say that the disembodied footsteps some sensitive students have reported belong to Ms. Heater. The footsteps echo with the "click-click" of high-heeled shoes that approach students then stop as if listening…or waiting? Feelings of impending doom have overcome some as they navigated the school's haunted hallways. None have stuck around long enough to see what might happen next, as they said the bell rang about then.

Chopticon High School *Photo from author's collection.*

An abandoned homestead. *Photo from author's collection.*

Some claim the haunting is all a fabrication of overactive teenage hormones or, if real, are unconnected to Heater's tragedy. Native Americans also lived and died on these lands. Did they leave a part of themselves behind? The area has been settled by Europeans for almost four centuries, and their lives have surely left a mark as well.

If there is some unfinished business related to the devoted but deceased teacher, rest in peace, Ms. Heater. You surely deserve it.

HAUNTED PRIVATE HOMES, TOBACCO BARNS, ETC.

The following represents some of the stories passed along from residents of the tri-county area. The locations described are all private property, and I've respected the owners' privacy and appreciate their willingness to share their experiences.

There's a section of what's affectionately referred to as the Seventh District in Saint Mary's County that has a long history of haints and spectral sights. The hot spot begins in Bushwood, Maryland, and moves on to points south. The owner of one old home, Lowton Hall (built circa 1913), has reported numerous paranormal activities there. He's heard the sound of frolicking children when no (mortal) children were present. A lady in a white dress often appears, as does a man with a black top hat. The lady appears only at the door of the master bedroom and is always attired in a filmy white gown as if prepared for bed. She stares at you as if confused by your presence in her home. Lamps have been turned over, pictures twisted askew and doors slammed of their own accord.

Not far from this home, another resident says a grandmother's home has experienced similar activity. In the home, built in 1936, spectral figures have been seen in the attic—along with frequent feelings of dread. A deceased aunt has been seen at night, and in broad daylight as well…only to disappear as suddenly as she appeared. A resident's mother has reassured her child after the mother's passing.

There's a home where a well-loved family dog still occasionally jumps in bed with the owners…years after its death.

Around another corner, a family barn stands where a young lad saw his brother after the young teenager drowned. Only thirteen years old, one must assume he had unfinished business or wanted to say his last goodbyes. Haunted tobacco barns are not entirely rare in the southern counties,

Above: Collapsed brick fireplace. Family legend says the wife of the author's ancestor was found deceased inside. *Photo from author's collection.*

Left: Tobacco barn. *Photo from author's collection.*

either. Considering the number of man-hours spent laboring over the crop and the accidents and deaths resulting from falls off the upper tiers, this isn't surprising.

I met a young lady in a governmental office a while back. She was a self-described sensitive, and we chatted amicably during our interminable bureaucratic wait. She told me of a haunted house on Ward Road in Dunkirk, Maryland, that she'd been brave enough to visit it as a child.

She approached the front door with her dog on a leash, and the canine stopped abruptly in the driveway in front of the deserted house and wouldn't advance. She coerced the dog forward, but again it balked at the steps to the porch and growled at the door opening. She tied the pup's leash to a bush beside the porch and cautiously stepped inside. She said she felt immediate discomfort and stress but forged ahead. Ahh, the persistence of youth....

Inside the house, antique dolls were scattered around in positions simulating torture. Some were cut up, and most had heads and limbs ripped away. She soon joined her dog outside and didn't visit again. I was unable to locate the house; I suspect it may have been destroyed, as many new homes have been built in the area. I wonder if the new residents have experienced any bumps in the night.

I regret that I didn't obtain the lady's name when her number was finally called before us, but I wanted to share her tale here. If you read this, I appreciate you sharing your story with my wife and me.

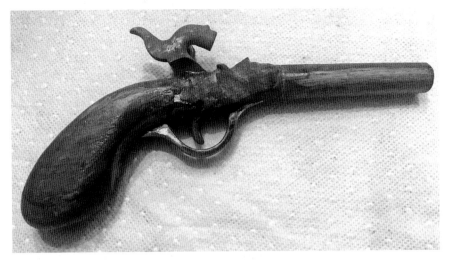

Flintlock Muff Pistol (circa 1780–1820) converted to percussion (likely post–Civil War) found buried by abandoned house. Grip and faux barrel added for display. *From author's collection.*

Hollywood Volunteer Rescue Squad is said to be haunted by a former member. Figures have been seen, and photographs have revealed unexplainable orbs.

There's an older home in Mechanicsville, Maryland, that's said to be haunted by the ghost of a bank robber. The legend says the robbery occurred in Baltimore in the early 1920s. The man almost made good his getaway but was shot by a bank guard. Sometime later, the farm owner observed a large contingent of vultures circling and landing at the edge of one of his fields. Upon investigation, he discovered the partially decomposed body of the thief (identified during an autopsy). Weird noises and footsteps also mark this haunting, which began about a decade after the robbery. This one may have a happy ending, as just after the millennium, the spirit is said to have whispered, "I got to go now." And with that, the paranormal activity is said to have ceased.

CRYPTOZOOLOGY

Even though many of the following are represented in diverse cultures throughout the world, I hesitated to include the reports of creatures in the category of cryptozoology. For the unfamiliar, cryptozoologists are committed to the search for and study of animals whose existence is disputed or unsubstantiated. For Southern Marylanders, this includes stories like the "Goatman," the "horned serpent," "Chessie" the sea serpent and the creature reported in Hollywood, Maryland cemeteries that resembles some of the lore of the Snallygaster. These are reported rarely enough but do have some historical reference by way of petroglyphs and pictographs and so merit inclusion here. They might also serve to illustrate the uncertainty of modern life even better than the witches, ghosts and demons we've covered. It would seem that the manifestations of our fears have come full circle. The "wendigo" and the "little people" could easily fit in this category.

THE **GOATMAN** IS THE subject of a story that's been circulating in an area of Waldorf (Charles County) and the back roads of Calvert County for a while. He's also been known to travel north to Prince George's County and has been reported in the Bowie area. His appearances had dwindled until a 1970s resurgence, when he was revived as a "scapegoat" for animal killings—the first of which was a family's dog, its head neatly severed from its neck.

Goatman is a satyr-like creature. Its top half is that of a horned and bearded man, while its bottom half resembles a goat—hooves and all. The creature's origin is vague. Some say it is the result of genetic engineering (alien DNA experiments, perhaps?) gone wrong, or a creature spawned from the depths of hell after some sadistic satanic ritual.

The Goatman has been reported in other states, including Alabama, Wisconsin, Texas and Kentucky. It is likely that its recurrence is attributable to teens reviving this relished story of a creature that attacks young couples in compromising positions at local lover's lanes. Oh, and did I mention that Goatman wields a mean (and bloody) axe?

Goatman has appeared on the national stage in both the *Hell Boy* and *X-Files* comics.

STORIES AND SIGHTINGS OF **Chessie** have circulated perhaps since the first colonists sought our shores aboard the *Ark* and the *Dove*. The idea of sea serpents was well known to them and always on their minds when at sea. The first reported sighting in modern times was by a helicopter pilot in the 1930s. There was a rash of sightings in the late 1970s through the 1980s.

Chessie is described as a reptilian creature at least twenty-five feet long, in the tradition of Nessie—the famous sea creature from Loch Ness in Scotland. It is postulated by believers that the animal is a throwback to an aquatic dinosaur, while scientists have dismissed the slim photographic evidence as depicting eels, river otters, manatees or possibly a released anaconda. As Chessie hasn't been known to cause any destruction or gobble up any small children or farm animals, we may well dismiss the latter.

I WAS A YOUNG man when I first heard of the **horned serpent**. Honestly, I laughed it off—as well I might. Who ever heard of a snake with horns, after all? The young boy who described the reptile to me was known for his honesty, and although I doubted his story, I didn't doubt his belief in it...so I reined in my laughter until I was beyond his hearing.

It was many years after this before I heard a similar report, and it was recounted by a different young man in his mid-twenties. He was walking in the woods in the central part of Saint Mary's County, very close to the original sighting. He claimed the horned snake was as big around as a man's lower arm and its total length as long as a man is tall. The snake worked its way through a honeysuckle thicket and didn't allow a good enough look at its entirety to provide more precise dimensions. About the horns, though, he had no doubts. When he saw the slinking movement, he tossed a stick in the snake's direction, and the reptilian head swirled about and stared. Perhaps it was a copperhead with opened mouth ready to strike and with its fangs exposed? Was it the snake's fangs they mistook for horns from fear-induced disorientation?

Southeastern Woodland Indians and the tribes around the Great Lakes believed in a horned serpent. They decorated pottery and made pictographs featuring its image. The creature was associated with inclement weather: rain, lightning and thunder. Mesopotamian and European cultures used horned serpents as cult fetishes, especially during periods of Roman occupation. Has the ancient symbol found life in Southern Maryland?

SOUTHERN MARYLAND IS AMONG the areas of many states and countries reporting the presence of a **Bigfoot** creature, or Sasquatch. The name *Sasquatch* predates European presence here and is an Anglicization of a Native American term.

Casts have been taken of abnormally large footprints, hair samples have been reviewed for DNA and photographs have been investigated. Although many questions have been raised, no solid evidence has been brought forward. Believers say nothing less than a Bigfoot corpse will satisfy naysayers.

The multiple names this cryptid is called is the best evidence of its existence: Almas in Mongolia, Yowies in Australia, Skunk ape in the Georgia and Florida swamps and Grassman in Ohio. Yeti is the name the legendary creature is tagged with in the Himalayan and Siberian regions of East Asia. Obviously, Bigfoot is far from a localized phenomenon, and that distinction is what separates it from other cryptids. They've been reported in just about every environment, Antarctica being the probable exception. They've been reported in every land that mankind has stepped foot in for as long as our species could vocalize what their eyes beheld. In Southern Maryland, the creatures have been sighted in the woods of all three counties. Several of our state parks are known hot spots, but I hesitate to identify them here. If such an animal does exist, it obviously prefers to be solitary and deserves its privacy.

One anonymous observer told me his story of an encounter with the beast. Camping on a hilltop near the Patuxent River, he heard a large animal running across the hill and in his general direction. The animal stopped, then ran again as another set of footfalls raced toward it. A longtime hunter, the man heard a grunt as a deer might make, then a rustling in the brush that sounded like the deer had abruptly changed direction, followed by a squeal of pain or fear. A sharp popping noise indicated to him that the deer's neck had been snapped. Silence followed, but for only a moment, as the larger animal move away down the hill and toward the river.

The next day, he investigated, but only drag marks and a few hairs marked the site of the life-and-death struggle. At the river's edge, he observed a trail of very large bare footprints in the sand. A big man would of course have big feet...but walking barefoot on the wet sand in subzero winter temps? Unlikely, I'd say, but people are sometimes strange. Still, what man could catch a running deer and snap its neck like a toothpick?

The large, hairy, bipedal man-ape has been called the missing link by some Bigfoot buffs. We know that such a creature did exist, at least once upon a time. The nearly ten-foot-tall *Gigantopithecus* is the likely candidate and is thought to have existed alongside our ancestor *Homo erectus*.

A modern study called epigenetics is proving that some ancestral experiences, although not coded in our DNA, are actually passed on to the following generations. Are these inherited memories of an interaction with *Gigantopithecus* the root cause of Bigfoot sightings? Or does the belief that something is real make it the explanation that our minds cling to when faced with the unexplainable? Or maybe, just maybe, an eight-to-ten-foot hairy ape-man still roams our swamps and river bottoms today. Maybe Bigfoot *is* real?

AS THE **SNALLYGASTER** IS mentioned below, and because it's probably the most infamous and indigenous of the Maryland cryptids, I'll add a bit about it. I'll note, however, that I've found no reference to any sightings in Southern Maryland. If anyone has, I'd love to hear from you about it. Snallygaster sightings are primarily relegated to the mountain counties of Western Maryland, with some reports in the central areas of the state. The beast is a bipedal, winged, half-reptile and half-bird hybrid that was first reported in the 1700s. Its tale—if not the creature itself—is thought to have arrived with German immigrants. It was popularized again in the early 1900s by the *Middletown Valley Register* in an effort to increase readership.

I'M NOT SURE WHAT to call the next entry, because I've seen no mention of it outside of local accounts. For lack of other references, I'll name the beast the **Saint John's Batman**. It's similar in form and action to the Snallygaster from the mountain counties, but unlike that cryptid, it's not a reptilian creature. It's comparable in size and abilities to the Mothman of Point Pleasant, West Virginia. The Batman, however, has no mythology or paranormal activity associated with it, and it is mammalian rather than insectoid.

One fan of the paranormal assures me that the Batman was once written up in a magazine devoted to cryptozoology and lesser-known "monsters," but I've found no reference to it in my research. I was, however, lucky enough to find an eyewitness account of one encounter with the beast. My witness advised that she and several friends had visited a cemetery in Hollywood, Maryland, one dark and cold winter night in the mid-1970s. They assured me they'd engaged in no mischief but had sat in the warm vehicle telling tales about school and boys. No one (living or dead) and no "thing" should have been disturbed by their presence.

In the meager light of a crescent moon, one of the girls spotted something moving in the shadows of the surrounding woods. Thinking it might be an owl, she pointed it out to her friends, but the creature grew to a considerable height as it climbed up to perch on a large marble tombstone. The creature stood frozen in place, its claws digging into the carved rock. Like a statue it watched them, so much so that they began to doubt what they'd just seen. The giant winged creature could easily be part of the stone monument as it continued to glare unmoving.

Mention was made of the Batman's glowing eyes. Its wings remained tucked away and folded as it watched the young women squirm in discomfort. They exchanged hasty glances, passing unspoken communication to go and to go now.

Before the driver could turn the key in the ignition, the creature unfurled its wings and leapt from the stone. It soared over their car and disappeared into the woods surrounding the city of the dead. It could be like the church gargoyles of old that protected the sacred places from evil. Does this creature now guard the resting places of those who've gone before us? Or does its appearance mirror the tragedies associated with the Mothman's arrival? Is the Batman foretelling an imminent disaster?

CONCLUSION

Boeing F/A-18s, P-8s and Lockheed Martin's Joint Strike Fighter share the Southern Maryland skies with eagles, hawks and waterfowl. On our bays and rivers, large ships and powerful motorboats have largely replaced the sails and paddles of yesteryear. A rural population of uniformity and familiarity has transformed itself into a culture of diversity, a true melting pot. Trying to hold back the onslaught of time is a fool's errand, but the wistful wanderings of nostalgia are inherently and uniquely human. And isn't it with our thoughts, dreams and memories that we name our spirits…our souls that will follow us when we depart this physical world?

Many of us still throw salt over our shoulders, steer away from black cats, handle mirrors with the utmost care and are especially cautious every Friday the thirteenth, but of course, it's out of habit, not fear. Thank goodness we've risen above the superstitious hysterias of our ancestors. Their myths, legends and ghost stories may provide a chill or two around a dying campfire, but our modern world is logical and rational. We've been told there's "nothing to fear except fear itself." We have switches on our walls to dispel the darkness and flashlights if the power happens to go out. Electronics protect our homes from unwanted intrusions, and a well-trained police force is but a phone call away.

Still, the innate desire to be frightened is programmed into our DNA. We invent new scares when the old ones cease to terrify us. Stories of Bigfoot and alien abductions dance in our dreams and perhaps engender a nervous laugh on waking. But are they any less real in our collective consciousness

Painted rock found outside of the Leonardtown, Maryland library. After three hundred years, people still remember Moll Dyer's tragic tale. *Photo from author's collection.*

than our ancient frights? The cinematic overload of cryptozoologists and ancient astronaut theorists replaced the demon hunters and séances of the past. The ghosts and haunts of bygone times were forgotten when such beliefs were explained away.

We've never been touched by an unseen hand or awakened to see a shadowy figure watching us in our sleep. Never has a voice been heard in which the speaker didn't stand before us, and ethereal mists have never passed us by on a moonlight walk. We're above all that foolishness today—aren't we?

BIBLIOGRAPHY

The material in this book has been drawn from many sources, published and online. As a native, "born and bred" Southern Marylander, however, most of these tales are familiar to me from conversations with other locals over the course of a lifetime. These are the personal recollections and experiences of longtime residents as well as the oral traditions of their families. These were their times and places…their echoes of the past.

The referenced sources served as a refresher of these conversations and memories and fleshed out portions of the stories I was less familiar with. I've included historical facts in every case, but of course, the subject matter and the testimony of witnesses can be very subjective.

References

Baltrusis, Sam. *Ghosts of Salem, Haunts of the Witch City*. Charleston, SC. The History Press, 2014.

Boyd, Rick. *Many Served in WWII. Some Didn't Come Back*. California, MD: The Enterprise, 2016.

Pogue, Robert E.T. *Old Maryland Landmarks*. Bushwood, MD: Self-published, 1972.

Potyraj, John E. *Common Bond—Saint Mary's Church, Bryan Town, Maryland*. Steeple Press, 1993.

Thompson, David W. *Sister Witch: The Life of Moll Dyer.* Farmington, MO. Solstice Publishing, 2017.

Varhola, Michael. *Ghosthunting Maryland.* Cincinnati, OH: Clerisy Press, 2009.

Wennerston, John. *The Oyster Wars of Chesapeake Bay.* Centreville: Maryland Tidewater Publishing, 1981.

Web Pages

"About Doctor Mudd." The Doctor Mudd House Museum. Accessed February 2019. http://drmudd.org/about-dr-mudd.

Cipolloni, Donna. "Haunted 409." NAS Patuxent River Tester. October 2015. Accessed February 2019. www.dcmilitary.com/tester/news/local/haunted/article_2f7ecc8c-4440-5e4b-818a-8d60223f456a.html.

Darago, Connie. "Still Lighting the Way." Bay Weekly Online. July 2000. Accessed February 2019. http://bayweekly.com.

Evans, Suzy, PhD. "James Madison, the Potomac Oyster Wars and the Constitutional Convention." History Chef. Accessed October 2018. http://lincolnslunch.blogspot.com/2010/07/james-madison-potomac-oyster-wars-and.html.

"The Ghost Fleet of Mallows Bay." Sometimes Interesting Blog. April 2013. Accessed October 2018. https://sometimes-interesting.com.

Higgins, David. "The Haunting of Chopticon High." Southern Maryland Chronicle. October 2018. Accessed March 2019. www.southernmarylandchronicle.com.

Historic Sotterley. Accessed October 2018. https://www.sotterley.org.

Long, Kat. "The Assassination of Abraham Lincoln." Smithsonian Institute. April 2015. Accessed February 2019. https://www.smithsonianmag.com.

"Maryland and World War I." The United States World War I Centennial Commission. Accessed November 2018. https://worldwar1centennial.org.

"Point Lookout State Park." Maryland DNR. Accessed November 2018. http://dnr.maryland.gov.

"Real Haunts." Maryland Haunted Houses. Accessed December 2018. https://www.marylandhauntedhouses.coms.

Ricksecker, Mike. "First Person: A Haunting Impression of the Mudd House." *Baltimore Sun*, October 2011. Accessed February 2019. https://www.baltimoresun.com.

Shaw, Benjamin. "Witch Hunts in the DC Area." Boundary Stones Blog. July 2015. Accessed February 2019. https://blogs.weta.org/boundarystones.

Skinner, Amy. *Historic Sites Context Study & National Register Evaluation for Calvert County*. MIHP Form. Accessed February 2019. https://mht.maryland.gov/secure/medusa/PDF/Calvert/CT-25.pdf.

Taylor, David. *Doctor Mudd House Pictures*, Boothie Barn Blog. Accessed January 2019. https://boothiebarn.com.

Varhola, Michael O. "People Report Various Paranormal Phenomena at Piney Point Lighthouse." America's Haunted Roadtrip. Accessed February 2019. http://americashauntedroadtrip.com.

"War of 1812." Destination Saint Mary's. Accessed January 2019. https://destinationsouthernmaryland.com.

Public Sites Mentioned

Adam's Tap-house & Grille
2200 Solomons Island Road South
Prince Frederick, MD 20678

Calvert Marine Museum
14200 Solomons Island Road South
Solomons, MD 20688

Dr. Samuel A. Mudd House Museum
3725 Doctor Samuel Mudd Road
Waldorf, MD 20601

Greenwell State Park
25420 Rosedale Manor Lane
Hollywood, MD 20636

Historic St. Mary's City
Visitor Center
18751 Hogaboom Lane
St. Mary's City, MD 20686
https://hsmcdigshistory.org

Mallows Bay Park
1440 Wilson Landing Road
Nanjemoy, MD 20662

Piney Point Lighthouse Museum & Historic Park
44720 Lighthouse Road
Piney Point, MD 20674

Point Lookout State Park
Park Headquarters
11175 Point Lookout Road
Scotland, MD 20687

Sotterley Plantation
44300 Sotterley Lane, PO Box 67
Hollywood, MD 20636
http://www.sotterley.org

St. Clement's Island Museum
38370 Point Breeze Road
Colton's Point, MD 20626

ABOUT THE AUTHOR

D avid W. Thompson is a local to the area written about here, and the tales are well known to him. The recent transitions in the community he's witnessed firsthand. David is the author of several historical fiction books and especially enjoys researching and writing paranormal history.

His first book in the "Legends of the Family Dyer" trilogy is *Sister Witch: The Life of Moll Dyer*, a historically accurate portrayal of the period and the daily lives of the Maryland colony in the late 1600s, flavored with paranormal seasoning. The second in the series is *His Father's Blood*. It traces the Southern Maryland to Kentucky migration of 1785 and the lives and times of both groups. It includes many of the fables and legends associated with those times and places. The last entry in the trilogy is *Sons and Brothers*. It's set in the modern era and reunites the family—from the mountains of West Virginia to the Southern Maryland coast (and of course, Moll Dyer makes a cameo appearance). David is both appreciative and humbled by the numerous awards won by this series.

The author enjoys kayaking on the flat-water rivers near home as well as the more vigorous waterways in the mountains. Such times afloat are his favorite moments spent with his wife and family.

His other creative pursuit is wood carving, for which he's received awards. He's a gardener (but lacks his father's expertise and devotion) and an amateur winemaker. He uses home-grown native fruits—elderberry, persimmon and Maryland's largest indigenous fruit, pawpaw.

Dave is a member of Maryland Writer's Association and the St. Mary's County Historical Society. He's easy to find on social media at:

https://www.dthompsonwrites.com
https://twitter.com/Thompson_DavidW
https://www.facebook.com/AuthorOfParanormal
https://www.goodreads.com/author/show/15425511.David_W_Thompson
https://www.amazon.com/dp/B076KR626G
Instagram@thompsondavidw